Notches of All Kinds

A Book of Timber Joinery

Canadian Cataloguing in Publication Data
Mackie, B. Allan (Bernard Allan), 1925-
Notches of all kinds

ISBN 0-920270-24-7 pa.

1. Timber Joints.　　2. Building, Wooden.　　3. House
construction. I. Title.
TH5662.M33　　　　694'.6　　　　C77-13179-4

Log House Publishing Company Ltd.,
Prince George, British Columbia, 1983.

First Edition 1977
Reprinted in paperback: 1983
© Log House Publishing Company Ltd.,
Post Office Box 1205, Prince George,
British Columbia, Canada, V2L 4V3.
ISBN 0-920270-24-7
Printed and bound in Canada.

CONTENTS

Notches

of

all

Kinds

A Book of
Timber Joinery

by B. Allan Mackie

INTRODUCTION

The good that has been wrought by the revival of
a purer taste in Architecture, and a recurrence to
better principles, is but the harbinger of the good
yet to be achieved.

— Raphael and J. Arthur Brandon, The
Open Timber Roofs of the Middle Ages

Perhaps 1977 is still too early to speak of the "Renaissance of Timber Building". But certainly we in Canada have at least two of the necessary conditions and a goodly part of the third, for a renaissance: we have had a noble beginning; we have suffered a decline that was nearly death; and we have revived at least the healthy outline of splendid things that may come.

Whether or not this healthy outline truly does forecast a new architecture worthy of being recorded as a renaissance is the particular concern of this book of timber joinery. With all my heart, I hope that this new generation of timber builders breaks through to new heights of skill and competence. For wherever they succeed, we all stand to gain in our total environment.

I know and accept the fact that men and women enter this profession with the expectation of profit-making which, for any art form, usually heralds its doom. It is not that the starving artist performs more brilliantly because of the hunger -- but rather, because he has so clear a vision of what he wants to do, that hunger is no longer relevant. It's the vision, the determination, the driving ambition to exercise a disciplined skill, that carries the artist to new heights ... and profit then occurs. It is this sequence that can be trusted to guard both the artist and the art form.

I am convinced, therefore, that if the new builders will hold firmly to a high standard of quality in their craft, they can safely take their well-earned gain and neither their craft nor their customers will suffer. If the new generation of builders proceeds on the workaday basic precepts of the mediaeval timber builders, who had very good wages, then we will indeed be entitled to speak with great pride of the Renaissance of Timber Building which, this time, will have its origin and base in Canada. To emulate those artisans, however, requires diligent, ongoing study and experiment.

The peak period of English woodwork, during the 15th and 16th centuries, knew their "carpenters" as experts in timber construction. By experts, as Crossley explains in "Timber Building in England", we mean "they had full control of the medium (usually oak) in which they worked, and appreciated its latent possibilities which they used to best advantage. Carpenters at that time knew that a trunk split with a riving iron preserved its vitality and strength better than sawing, and the use of naturally bent timber was more intelligent in the use of material than cutting curves by artificial means." Further ... "both carpenter and blacksmith made their own tools, which were commensurately valuable, as in the will of Randulph Penteney of Ixworth, Suffolk, in 1472, who willed his tools to his son."

Britain, as other European nations, enjoyed a long and gradual development in building so that experts could indeed ply their trade at a time when forests shrouded those lands. It was so in Canada, too, in the beginning, with the result that not only a stout kind of building style was established by both French and British, but some uniquely Canadian modifications developed, now called pièce-en-pièce or Red River frame.

But a society such as ours, which had its beginnings in the slavering exploitation of resources, has also established a precedent. Today, even the commercialization of air, drinking water, and beauty is acceptable. Efficiency, it was called, and became a watchword; profit became the motive; until we stood in danger of becoming a people from whom all artistic expression, if not sanity, had been steamrollered. And worse, we became willing and anxious to buy anything that was offered. We still stand in danger of collectively forgetting how it could be otherwise, and that the earth could be peaceful, clean, lovely.

It is too ugly to suggest that each cloud has a silver lining when certain clouds are drenched with materials which can rain upon the populace and hasten their deaths. Nevertheless, it was the ugly cloud of pollution that aroused society to the fact that we had lost more than we had gained. We suddenly realized there are at least two prices to be paid for manufactured goods: one in the purchase, the other in the loss from the face of the earth the resources which fed the production-line machinery.

I'd suggest that the Renaissance of Timber Building has had its beginnings in this realization of also a third price to be paid for instant packaged goods: the loss of human skills. In particular, we had almost forgotten how to build for ourselves.

The price of passive comfort has always been high, but now it is seen to be suicidal. If not curbed, there could be no clean air or water left to us, no timber, and a populace unfit to look after itself. But the instinct to survive is strong, and this awareness, coupled with the love for a good home that all humans have, is now setting the new direction for our work in Log Construction. We must still beware of those who would, as always, try to subject even these rare resources -- building timbers -- to some quick and easy packaging for instant housing, for they, too, are part of the problem.

But there is also a human instinct for artistic expression ... so that when all these healthy motives come together in the building of a log home, I believe there are few mediums for human creativity which give greater satisfaction.

As yet, this art form -- the timber building -- has not shown its permanent direction for the 20th century. It is in its beginning phase. We remain vastly inhibited by the influences of Europe where the craft reached such an exalted height in the middle ages, declining as resources diminished, until other priorities influenced the builders and patrons. We are, therefore, in a pioneering condition again, as the lost skills are redeveloped and new boundaries defined.

These boundaries must include such questions as how large a house should be; what is a Canadian style; what is the right size of timber to build with; what style of corner is to be used for what purposes; what is the most lasting design ... these questions, and many more, have still to be answered, modified, tested and retested, before the new direction fully emerges. This is the healthiest of processes. As long as the log builders' trade is flourishing, there will be new questions and new boundaries put forward.

In this process of developing a new architecture in log construction, each builder, whether good or bad, will contribute. Each log building has the opportunity to set a new standard. As each design is tested, a new parameter will be established, adding to the available knowledge. And as each year passes, time will prove the worth of each innovation.

This is not to say that the building traditions of Europe should be ignored ... such is definitely not my meaning. Often, in fact, I like to recall the exquisite excitement of those craftsmen who first conceived the idea of eliminating the tie beam, and who dared to execute this utterly new concept, thus creating for the first time the seemingly airborne and immensely beautiful hammer beam in roof construction. That was a triumph which has lived down through the ages to enrich us all ... but only because a superb skill could conceive a new breakthrough and had the courage to test it.

It is prudent to remember, too, that timber building in Europe reached a maturity and died; and that it is at this point we begin again. We are the younger generation ... the sons who may have inherited a few tools, a few drawings, a few shards of recorded history. While we are aware of the accomplishments of the parent entity, the decision at this time is entirely our own as to whether we will equal them ... surpass them ... or whatever. It is the purpose of this book to suggest we learn all that history can teach us, resolving to carry forward within this noble tradition but in a new direction.

Change in direction sometimes takes place because of changing conditions. It is encouraging that as little as six years ago when I wrote my first book, the general conception of a log house had deteriorated so pitifully that it was considered to be a small makeshift shelter built far off in some swamp by a gnarled old gentleman wearing buckskin underwear. The most that was generally expected of such a building was that it should keep out some of the wind, most of the rain, and all of the wolves. A large part of my work in both writing and teaching has been to destroy that "cabin" concept, in order to build correctly. Luckily, this has in large part been achieved and the direction has changed drastically, reaching the present general state in which thousands upon thousands of people again see a log house as the ultimate in good quality construction.

So because of this changed and upgraded direction, untold hundreds of log homes have been built across this land. And within this process can be seen all the elements of our future progress, and from which we must again choose: some of the buildings are small and poor while many are large and ambitious; some show the scars of the machine age or of frantic speed in building, while others are well and carefully made. For my part, I believe that builders will stretch their skills and imaginations toward new and better heights just as long as these efforts are properly valued. Thus a climate of approval and encouragement is just as important as is the training and expertise of the builder.

The log construction skills have already revived to the point where the ultimate direction of our design and style may soon emerge. But it was, and will always be, necessary for builders to have explored and experimented and personally gained sufficient experience along with their basic training to be able to make responsible evaluations.

For many students, this has meant the discarding of learned and commonly accepted norms, such as those of frantic speed and less-then-perfect production-line quality which is a thinly disguised attempt to bring another sacrifice of resources to the feet of the gods of profit. But Nature has a nice way of demonstrating, in a surprisingly short time, what happens to violated trees. And sufficient numbers of handcrafted buildings were in place, for comparison, well ahead of these poor sawn things. Thus I can thankfully record I know of no builder who, once trained in the intelligent use of natural timber, has ever felt tempted to use factory methods. I am thankful, too, that society's raised level of consciousness generally supports him in this.

Because such tremendous advantages are to be gained for us all, environmentally, from the best work that log builders can do, I resolved to do this book consolidating most of the needed body of information. Even if I were to live another 100 years, it would be almost impossible to copy the teaching methods of the mediaeval timber builders who taught one apprentice, from childhood, in his life. Again, this is not to say their method is faulty, for it produced a competence that will remain a very lofty challenge to us all. But there are hundreds of builders today who are ready for instruction. And this book of timber joinery will be able to travel farther and faster, to last longer, and to spend more time with each builder than I can.

I have taught a great many of today's new generation of builders and I may be able to contribute another decade of active teaching, with perhaps a further decade beyond that in which to support and encourage a Renaissance of Timber Building. This, alone, is not enough. I have established a school so that students can study, then leave to gain experience, then return to study more. But new students are coming forward. And for that matter, a good builder is never finished learning.

Thus it seems time to put certain instructions into a more enduring form and so I have recorded this information about some of the notches and timber joins needed in log construction. Much of this data has been around a long time, but some of it is newly developed. So may I say, by way of encouragement to all timber builders, that in our newfound ability to record and to teach, we have already gained one great improvement over our gifted ancestors. Now, let us do them proud.

THE STRUCTURE OF WOOD

Before it is possible to make the best decision in the selection of a certain notch or joint for any particular application, consideration should be given to the physical makeup and properties of the wood to be used.

Species of wood differ greatly in respect to colour, odour, ornamental characteristics, weight, and mechanical properties. One of the most obvious differences between the species is in weight, which may vary from as little as 6 lbs. per cubic foot in an air-dry condition to as much as 80 lbs. The weight of those woods commonly used for building purposes in Canada will range from 24 to 50 lbs. per cubic foot in a dry condition.

In spite of the great differences in weights, the various species are remarkably similar in their chemical makeup. Chemical analyses of wood will show that wood which weighs 50 lbs. per cubic foot is made up of essentially the same ingredients as wood weighing half as much. Therefore, the difference in weight must be explained by differences in the structural systems or arranging the wood substances within a given species.

Wood is composed of tiny cells packed so closely together that they can be seen only with the aid of strong magnification. The thickness of these cell walls determines the density of the wood, woods which have thin walls being light and those with thick walled cells being heavier. It is obvious, therefore, that the various ways in which the elements of wood are arranged must have an important bearing on the uses to which each species is suited. Thus it will be to the great advantage of builders to consider the important aspects of wood structure upon which the properties and, as a consequence, the uses of the different woods must depend.

Woods are grouped into two classes commonly designated as softwoods and hardwoods. These terms are not strictly accurate since some hardwoods are softer than some softwoods. But the structure of the wood is typical in each of these classes and is responsible for such differences in physical properties as to make them readily identifiable as suited to certain purposes.

Generally, the so-called softwoods are conifers, classified in a group called Gymnosperms, a term broadly signifying plants bearing exposed seeds (usually cones). The pines and spruces are well known examples of Gymnosperms.

The other group, comprised of the various orders of hardwoods, consists of Angeosperms, which have true flowers, and seeds enclosed in a fruit. All the Canadian softwoods have needle-like or scale-like leaves which, except for the larches, persist throughout the winter. The broad-leafed trees (hardwoods) are deciduous although in some cases the dead leaves remain on the tree for some time before falling and, in one case (Arbutus), the tree sheds its bark rather than its leaves.

On the outside of the wood portion of the tree -- between the wood and the bark -- is a thin layer of living tissue called the Cambium layer. The inside of this layer of tissue has the ability to deposit new layers of wood each year on the trunk of the tree, while the outside of the Cambium layer produces the bark. This layer of new wood which is produced each year in a healthy tree forms concentric application around the centre of the tree. The cells formed in the spring and early summer are thin-walled and have larger openings than the wood formed later in the year which is characterised by a thicker-walled and darker layer of wood ... hence the so-called "annual" rings.

Since strength is dependent upon the weight of wood, wood with finer annual rings and a greater proportion of summer wood as opposed to spring wood, will be the stronger.

As the tree becomes larger, some of the cells of the inner wood are sealed off so that sap no

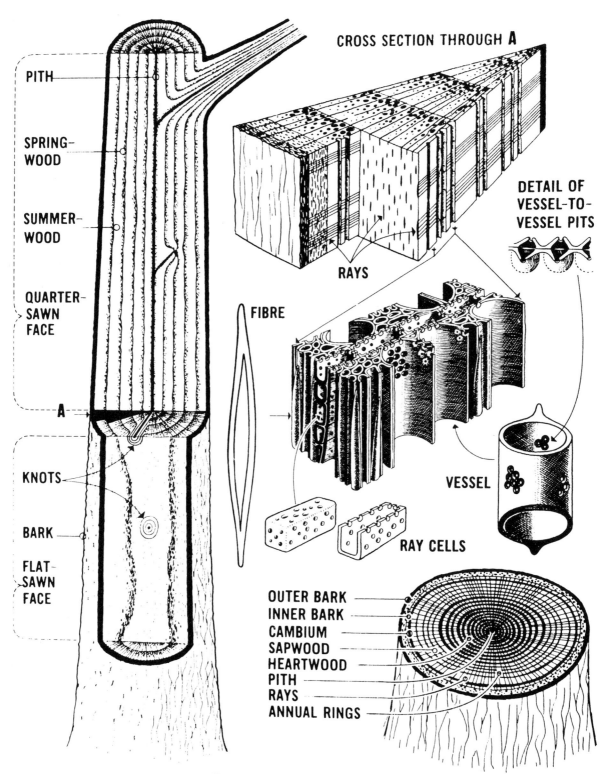

PITH

SPRING-
WOOD

SUMMER-
WOOD

QUARTER-
SAWN
FACE

A

KNOTS

BARK

FLAT-
SAWN
FACE

CROSS SECTION THROUGH A

RAYS

DETAIL OF
VESSEL-TO-
VESSEL PITS

FIBRE

VESSEL

RAY CELLS

OUTER BARK
INNER BARK
CAMBIUM
SAPWOOD
HEARTWOOD
PITH
RAYS
ANNUAL RINGS

THE STRUCTURE OF WOOD

longer passes through it and up the tree. This wood is called "heartwood". The heartwood of most trees is more resistant to decay than is the sapwood. For this reason, then, hewn logs are often more resistant to decay than round logs.

Hardwoods are different in cell structure to softwoods, in that their wood is composed of vessels of considerable length as compared to the short cells of Tracheids in the softwoods. These vessels also have a thin-walled structure in the springwood and a thicker wall in the summerwood. They are so fine, in some species, that they are difficult to see without a microscope.

Under certain conditions trees will produce an abundance of thick-walled cells in one part of the tree. This is known as Compression Wood and is generally formed to provide additional support to a leaning tree. At the base of most limbs, compression wood is also to be found. If this condition is present in quantity, the timber will be subject to excessive checking and warping.

Wood of a freshly-felled tree may be more than one half water, by weight, or said to have 100% moisture content. The equilibrium moisture content (i.e., when the wood and the surrounding air are of the same moisture content) in many places in Canada is about 12% so if a lower content is required, the wood will have to be exposed to artificial heat. Some builders who have had too-handy access to sawmill facilities have experimented with kiln-drying whole logs with disastrous effects. It is to overcome the problems of drying -- rather than of insulation -- that some machine-made "kit" manufacturers of so-called log houses have gone so far as to hollow out the logs and re-fill them with foam insulation. Anyone with a good understanding of the structure of a tree, however, will perceive that logs must follow natural, albeit slow, ways of drying, to achieve the best results.

Wood does not begin to shrink until the moisture content is reduced below the fibre saturation point -- which is the condition of the wood when there is just sufficient moisture to saturate the cell walls but with no moisture in the cell cavity. Above the fibre saturation point, the additional water is stored in the cell cavity and produces no change in the wood volume; but below the fibre saturation point, water is removed from the cell walls with a relative reduction in wood volume resulting.

The fibre saturation point seems to be about

25% moisture content. Therefore in drying logs down to an equilibrium moisture content of 12%, shrinkage is bound to occur. What is of concern here, to the builder, is that the outside of the log will reach the fibre saturation point earlier than the interior of the log does; thus it will begin to shrink earlier; and checking is a direct result of this phenomenon. So it is apparent, therefore, that if checking is to be avoided, evaporation must be slowed and controlled. Thus, under certain conditions it may be advisable, for example, to leave the bark on the log as long as possible to provide a damp covering. There are other ways of slowing down the exterior drying, but the basic principle must always remain that winter-cut wood provides the best answer to this problem.

Because shrinkage is due to the contraction of the cell walls, shrinkage causes a reduction in the cell diameter but does not appreciably affect the cell length. The reason for this is that the individual particles comprising the cell walls are made up of long crystals arranged, for the most part, parallel to the long axis of the cell. In the growing tree, water is present as a film between the crystals so when the wood dries, the water is removed and the component crystals draw closer together, therefore the cell shrinks much more in diameter than in length. Shrinkage, also, is not equal in all directions across the grain; it is greatest in circumference and least in diameter.

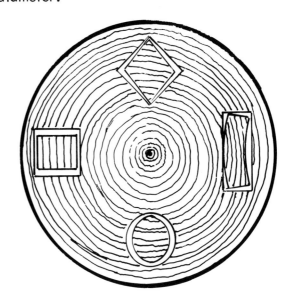

Diagram illustrating the shrinkage of wood across the grain.

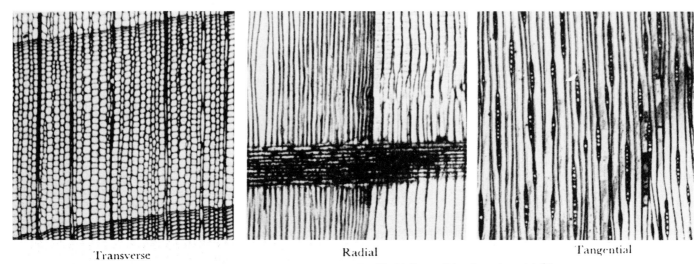

| Transverse | Radial | Tangential |

Western hemlock — *Tsuga heterophylla* (Raf.) Sarg. Wood sections × 50

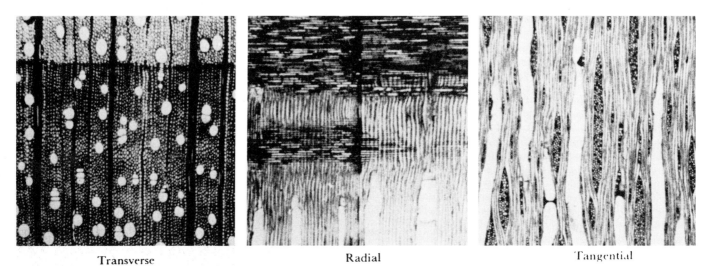

| Transverse | Radial | Tangential |

Sugar maple — *Acer saccharum* Marsh. Wood sections × 50

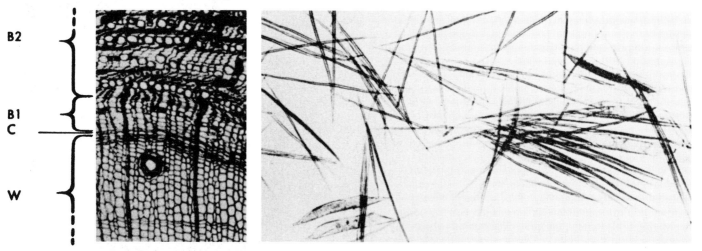

B2

B1
C

W

White pine (*Pinus Strobus* L.)
W—wood   C—cambium   B1—inner bark,
B2—collapsed bark.   Transverse × 50

Cells of white birch (*Betula papyrifera* Marsh.) × 25.
Wood was placed in acid which attacks cementing
bond thereby allowing the component cells to separate.

THE STRUCTURE OF WOOD

The permeability of wood -- its ability to accept moisture -- is another characteristic to be taken into consideration.

The sapwood portion of the tree has the greater ability to take on water and is therefore more subject to decay than the heartwood which has been sealed off from the active growth function of the tree and so is less permeable. These differences in the inner and outer parts of the tree were responsible for much of the hewing that was undertaken in early buildings. But with modern preservative treatment methods, the ability of the sapwood to accept moisture can be turned to good advantage as it provides access to the outer layers of wood for these liquid-carried preservatives. If an oil is the liquid to be used, all the better, since it will work to reduce the tendency of the sapwood to dry too quickly and consequently less checking will occur.

Most of the tests for thermal conductivity, to date, have begun from the premise that the wood in log construction is in the form of boards. There is genuine cause to doubt that such tests can be applied directly to round log construction. So, until more appropriate figures are produced, we can postulate that thermal conductivity will be related to the weight of the wood because of the cellular nature of the wood. Light woods, having thinner cell walls, consequently will have a greater ability to insulate.

There is such a wide range of opinion as to what constitutes an adequate size building log, that perhaps all one can state with assurance is that the larger the logs, the more insulating qualities they will possess. Wood is an excellent insulation material, therefore great wall thickness is not essential. But for a permanent and comfortable house in the Canadian climate, a mean diameter of 9 to 10 inches is a minimum size of log to aim for.

(For much of the foregoing information, I am indebted to CANADIAN WOODS, Their Properties and Uses, a text I have valued since my student days at Ranger School.)

TOOLS FOR NOTCHING

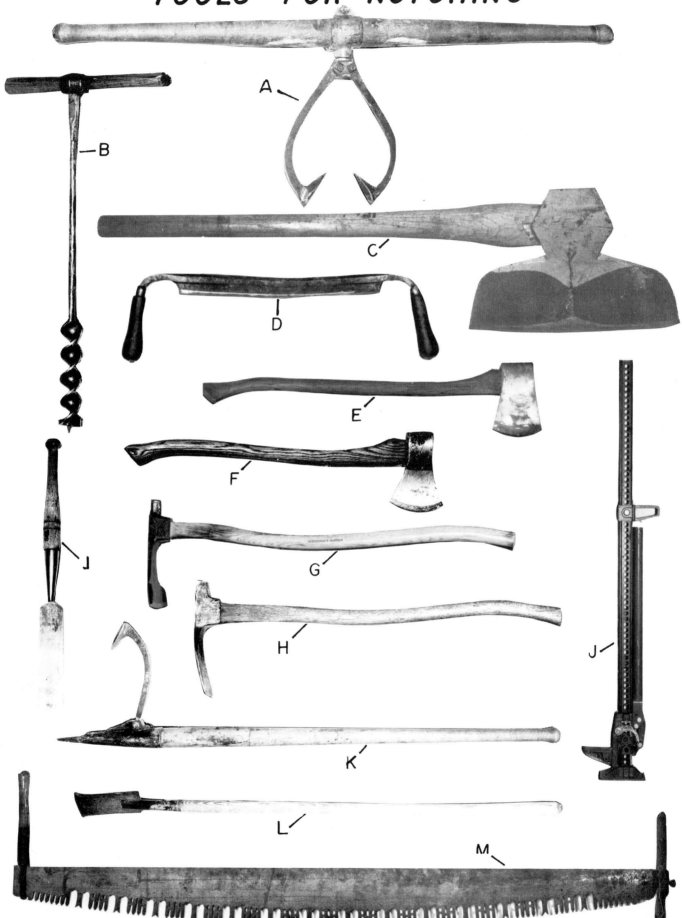

Tools, wrought by the blacksmiths of Europe and traded for furs, were perhaps one aspect of the white man's cultural impact upon the Indian and Eskimo of this continent which might have been called good ... might have been, had the tools been good. Certainly, the Eskimos and Indians were quick to assess the great value of basic tools which could provide a measure of relief from centuries of struggle. And if even those axes had been of the same superb quality as the beaver and otter skins being offered in exchange, what a story we might now share of those indigenous builders and carvers who might have freely expressed this sudden, dramatic release of artistic energy. Only the Haida, somewhat protected on the Queen Charlotte Islands, were able to achieve this ... and their brief period of work with timber buildings is a powerful statement of what might have been done. The tragedy (not just for the Indian and Eskimo people but for us all) is that most of the whiteman's trade tools were of shoddy quality which did little, if anything, to improve the lot of the customer no matter how diligently he tried to use them.

Often people bring to my log construction classes tools which are well made, beautiful to see and to use, and which are well-suited to the purpose for which they were designed. Usually, these implements are very old. And this always sets me to puzzling ... why, then, in olden times when such expertise was both possible and readily available, did our white ancestors foist shoddy tools onto trusting customers? And why -- even today when technology is a new kind of god and improvements upon almost anything are said to be possible -- are shoddy tools still being made and foisted off onto virtually everybody? When I see the strengthening of self-confidence, the all-around development of ability that comes to my students along with their learning to build, I begin to suspect I know the answer ...

The Eskimos and Indians were entirely correct in their original evaluation ... that a basic hand tool of superb quality is worth almost any price, for it provides the means of liberating oneself (even today) from the severest strictures of our environment. It is therefore a particular concern that the serious builder of today should follow another of the traditions of the mediaeval timber builder, who made his own tools. These proud workmen not only learned a complete command of the medium in which they worked, but valued their equipment so highly that these tools would be bequeathed to their sons. The builder of today, if he is to pick up successfully in that tradition, must set forth on his lonely pilgrimmage to find, to borrow, to buy, or to make his own set of log builder tools, at least knowing what is needed, as well as the quality and type of tool required.

Since power tools wear out, I have never to my own satisfaction been able to decide who is working for whom. I suspect, at times, that the man is working for the tool ... and I should like to begin this discussion with the chain saw. I must admit that I cannot, in good conscience, recommend any chain saw that is manufactured in North America to date. They are so vastly

A – timber carrier
B – 2" auger
C – 12 lb. broad axe
D – draw knife
E – 5½ lb. single bit axe
F – 3½ lb. oxhead axe
G – lip adze
H – timber adze
I – slick
J – Jack-all jack
K – 5 ft. peavey
L – peeling spud
M – bucking saw

1.   The Mackie scriber. Adjustable cutting scribers combined with dividers.
2.   Starrett #92 dividers modified to carry a horizontal level bubble.
3.   Starrett #92 dividers.
4.   Indelible pencil. Marks under most conditions and fits #92 dividers.
5.   Lumber crayon.
6.   Soft carpenter's pencil.

inferior to what is being made in Europe to-day that I am sure the only reason they can be sold at all is because we, like the Indian and Eskimo of the 18th century, are too well-mannered to resist properly. The North-American saw that has any stamina is so horribly noisy that it should be legislated against; the others are both noisy and of an inferior quality. The Paul Bunyan legend could never have flourished, had he been described as using one of these.

At this time, then, I can only recommend the Jonsered, Husqvarna, and Stihl saws of moderate sizes for the log builder. These operate quietly, and are as mechanically efficient as can be obtained now.

Large saws for log work -- for production work:

Jonsered   920

Husqvarna   181 C.D., 2100 C.D.

Stihl   056 Super

Moderate sized saw -- for good speed and all work:

Jonsered   630

Husqvarna   L65, 266 C.D., 61 C.D.

Stihl   032, 038

Small Saws for close work and finishing detail:

Jonsered   520

Husqvarna   44 C.D.

Stihl   020 AV

Above. Gasoline powered chain saw and the tools required to keep it cutting.

1 - Stihl 020 Professional. A very nice light chain saw of about 20 c.c. displacement. This one has a 16" bar and a $\frac{1}{4}$ pitch chain, and is equipped with a safety brake. Use it for finishing work and for any work in difficult or awkward positions.

2 - Bar wrench.
3 - Round file for chain.
4 - Raker file.
5 - Raker gauge.

Use a 16" or 20" bar with standard chipper chain. This is adequate for almost every situation. There are ripping chains and full chains for smooth work but the difference resulting from all this is of questionable value. The main component of quality logwork is, more certainly, the control exercised by the operator.

All these saws are available with a "chain-brake", a highly recommended safety feature which stops the chain instantly in case of kick-back.

The chain saw is probably the largest single expense encountered in acquiring log builder tools. Therefore it is satisfying to know that a good axe is still probably the most important implement that a builder can put his hand to. I wish that I could recommend a brand, or even a variety of brands, of axe which are good; but

again, this is not possible.

An oxhead axe, made in England, is good as a light axe (3½ lb.). A Swedish axe with the brand name of Advika is good as a heavy axe (5 or 5½ lb.). And Australian competition axes are good, if you can find one. But it remains my cherished hope, first expressed in the 2nd edition of BUILDING WITH LOGS, that I may someday be able, with confidence, to recommend to all my students the name of a tool manufacturer in Canada to whom they may direct their enquiries. Surely a good axe is not too much to ask of a highly industrialized economy? Yet we know that it is. So it may well be that it is a student who, one day, sets his hand to this most important aspect of the building trade. His name will surely be honoured by all those who need and value a basic working tool of the quality that can endure through a century.

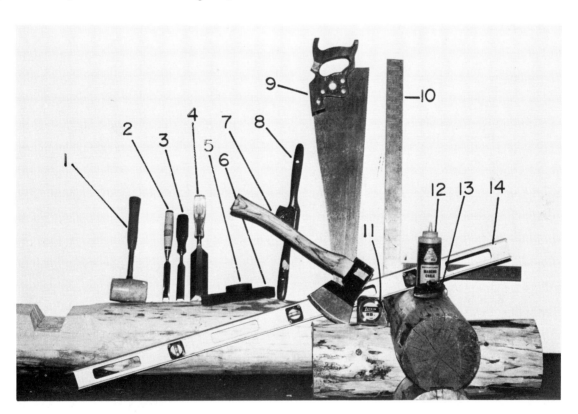

Above: a minimal set of carpenter's tools that the log builder will need.

1 – wood or hard rubber mallet
2 – 3/4" wood chosel
3 – 1" wood chisel
4 – 2" wood chisel
5 – round carborundum axe stone
6 – flat oil stone (coarse & fine)
7 – bench axe

8 – large spoke shave
9 – 8-point crosscut saw
10 – framing square
11 – 25' tape measure
12 – good supply of chalk powder
13 – chalk line
14 – 4' framer's level

NOTCHES
for
WALL LOGS

BLIND NOTCH FOR FIRST

It is often desirable to use a blind notch to conceal the end of the first ½ log in order to avoid the questionable appearance of a slabbed log protruding beyond the foundation. In order to construct this blind notch, place the half log on the foundation in the usual way, flatten the sill log slightly, and place it on the adjacent wall with the flat side down (1). When it is in position, draw a vertical centre line (a) on the end of the log with a level and scribe the notch (b) on both ends of the log.

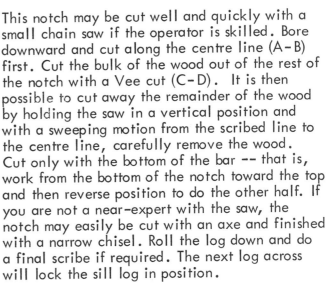

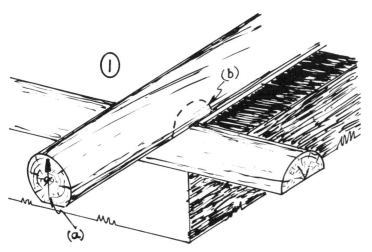

Turn the log over and join the centre lines previously drawn on the log ends, with a chalk line (2). The ½ log may be cut off on a corresponding centre line as indicated by the dotted line in Figure (2). Cut the ½ notch on the scribed line and chalk line but take care to cut the correct side.

This notch may be cut well and quickly with a small chain saw if the operator is skilled. Bore downward and cut along the centre line (A–B) first. Cut the bulk of the wood out of the rest of the notch with a Vee cut (C–D). It is then possible to cut away the remainder of the wood by holding the saw in a vertical position and with a sweeping motion from the scribed line to the centre line, carefully remove the wood. Cut only with the bottom of the bar -- that is, work from the bottom of the notch toward the top and then reverse position to do the other half. If you are not a near-expert with the saw, the notch may easily be cut with an axe and finished with a narrow chisel. Roll the log down and do a final scribe if required. The next log across will lock the sill log in position.

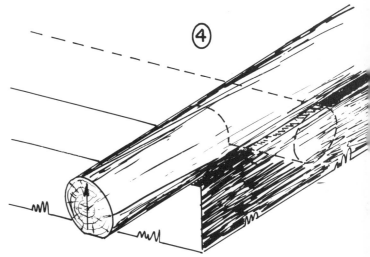

ROUND NOTCH

Method 1. Place the log to be fitted directly over the final position to which it will be fitted ("a" Fig. 1) and with the carpenter's level in a plumb position, mark the width of the log below on the side of the new log ("b"-"c"). Set the scribers to an opening which may be a little less than the amount of wood to be covered ("d").

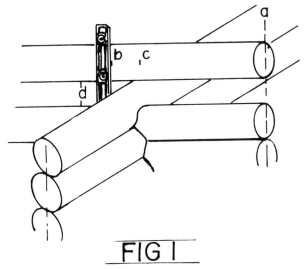

FIG 1

Align the scribers with mark b as in Fig. 2, and draw scribed line b-c. Start the scribe at the bottom and work to the midpoint at the top, from each side. Take care that the scribers are held in a perfectly vertical position while the line is drawn. The reference marks b-c will assist in this. Also be careful not to move the log until each end has been marked.

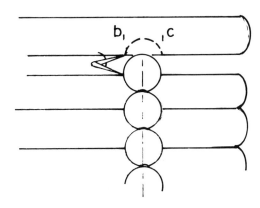

FIG 2

When this operation has been completed, the log may be rolled over to the inside of the building and the "rough notch" cut may be undertaken. If a chain saw is being used, make cut "f" first. This will give you a point to work to, and will allow the wood to break out more easily when cuts "d" and "e" have been made.

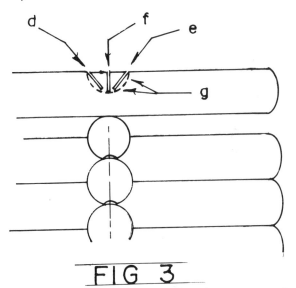

FIG 3

Start right at the line, to make the cuts, and end as near the line as possible. This cut may be made with an axe just as well, but I find many people lack the skill and stamina required. Whichever tool you choose, the danger of over-cutting is greatest at point "g". Cut "f" may be omitted if one is greatly skilled or if the logs are small. The remaining wood may be quickly removed with several shallow cuts with the chain saw("h", Fig. 4). Keep one side of the bar in the open (as in Photo #3) and a curve is possible.

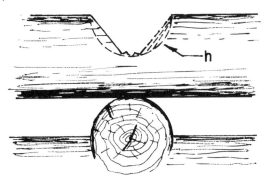

FIG 4

If this work is done with an axe, clean out the bottom of the notch first, then follow the scribed line with the tip of the axe and the handle high. This will give a sharp edge to the notch which will be easier to finish than if it were cut by holding the handle of the axe down and cutting with the heel of the blade. If you do this, you form a beveled edge and sometimes cut off the line before the interior of the notch is brought down to the required depth. If you find it awkward to use the tip of the axe, it may be better to cut down squarely with the axe until you are about $\frac{1}{2}$" away from the line, then cut around the line with a 3/4" chisel. This may be a little slower but will save time in the long run. Axemanship is a skill which one may well be proud of because it is not easily acquired. I have an admiration for the "hewers of wood" based on a personal knowledge of the devotion required to become one. It is, therefore, no disgrace to use a chisel until such time as your skill develops, as it surely will, to the point where you can employ an axe accurately in almost any capacity.

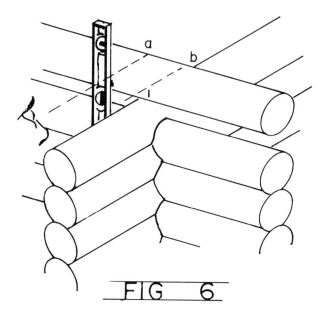

FIG 6

you are working on. Place this measurement on each side of the proposed notch. You now have points "a", "b", and "c" through which an accurate line may be drawn. Accuracy will improve with practice and when each end has been done, you may cut out the notch in the same way as before. You are now ready for a final scribe and a final notch.

FIG 5

Method II. If the building is small, it may be advantageous to place the log on the wall with the bow down and sketch the notch on the upper side. This is somewhat faster since the notch may be cut without again moving the log. Place the level as before, but this time place marks a and b on the top of the log (Fig. 6). It is a good idea to place marks on the **side of** the log at the same time to check accuracy.

Place the level across the top of the log and transfer the measure of "d" (Fig.7) to the log

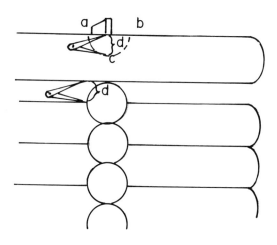

FIG 7

The work of scribing has been dealt with in my book, BUILDING WITH LOGS. A portion of that work is repeated here because scribing is so important a part of log building.

In the last year or so a great many kinds, shapes and sizes of scriber have made their appearances. This is all to the good and perhaps a better design will emerge.

The purpose of a pair of log scribers is to transfer

a predetermined measurement directly from one surface to an adjacent surface with a high degree of faithfulness. You will be transfering the shape of the upper side of the lower log to the surface of the log above, which is to be fitted.

The scribers, therefore, are similar to a pair of dividers. Dividers may be used for this purpose and a pair that is capable of holding a pencil are an advantage. (See "Tools".)

Whatever style of scriber you use, set the points to about the widest space between the two logs. This may be altered for a particular reason -- you may wish to scribe the log down farther to help keep the walls even; or you may, in some positions, wish to scribe less.

The scriber points are kept vertical -- that is, one point directly above the other and the handle is kept as near to a horizontal position as you can manage.

FIG 9

can create a fit that requires little insulation. The scribing of a log might take the beginner as much as an hour's time to complete, but it is time well spent. When the marking is done, the log should be rolled inward on the building, with the notches up, for this finishing work to be done. Keep in mind that the scribed line will still be visible when the waste wood has been removed from around the groove and notches.

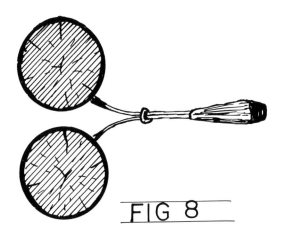

FIG 8

The scribed line is carried the length of the log (Fig. 8), up and over the notch, and continues to include the end of the log that protrudes to the outside of the wall (Fig. 9). Use the divider end for marking around the notch because the hooked ends will not function here (Fig. 10).

The whole idea of scribing is that the two lines so formed are a constant vertical distance apart at any two points which are one above the other ("x"-"y" Fig 11). Thus, by cutting away the intervening wood from the upper log it will drop to an exact fit on the log below.

Of late, a number of scribers have appeared with levels incorporated into them, which more dependably ensures the correct horizontal position. These can be very good, and can be a great help around the notch. Careful work

FIG 10

21

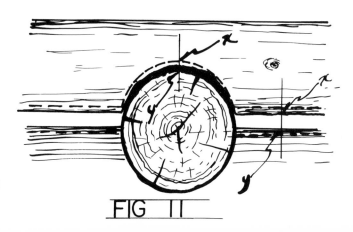

FIG II

When the scribed log has been rolled inward onto the building and the notch is now turned up, the scribed line should look much like Figure 12, with the dotted line "e" representing the mark left by the scribers. Care will have been exercised to ensure that this line is complete, otherwise each gap in this line is a length where you'll be uncertain where to cut, and it is very difficult to get the log back into its former position if you have forgotten to scribe some portion of the line.

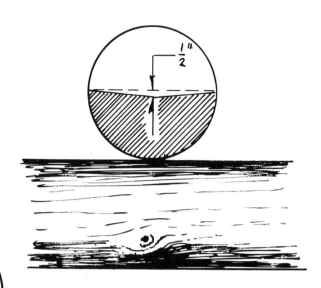

SECTION A-A

FIG 13

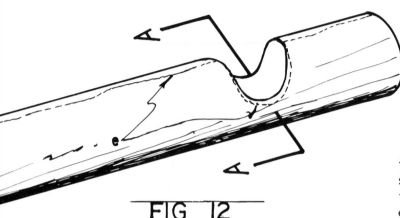

FIG 12

If the line is fully complete but appears too faint, trace over it with chalk or indelible pencil. In this way, it may be followed much more readily.

Cut into or "score" the scribed line around the notch with a very sharp knife. A banana or lino knife works well. Working carefully, cut about 3/16" deep, following the scribed line exactly, all around the notch. There is no need to do this along the lateral groove, however, as it serves no purpose there.

To finish the final notch, use either an axe, a chain saw, an adze, or a mallet and chisel. They all work well, depending on your skill. But my experience is that most people want to use a chain saw, so a chain saw cut will be described now in detail. Whichever tool you decide to use, the final cut should appear in section as in Fig. 13.

When using a chain saw, then, make the first cut in the centre of the notch about 1" wide and down to the scribed line (Fig. 14). This can be accomplished by allowing the blade to wobble, or it may be done by making several closely adjacent cuts that overlap. The saw should be positioned so that the bar is slightly more than halfway across the notch (section Fig. 14). The tip should be slightly lower than

the heel of the bar in order to obtain the slightly hollow profile required. However, keep this hollow very shallow, otherwise the strength of the corner will be diminished. Remember that at least 70 to 80% of the building weight must be carried on the corners, to prevent the displacement of wall logs. When too much weight is carried mid-span on a wall, particularly if the wall is in excess of 20 feet in length, the danger exists that a log can be squeezed out of position. This is a highly discouraging thing to have happen and, if any danger at all exists, the builder should peg the logs.

When the work has progressed to the point illustrated in Figure 14, the notch should be worked in quarters. Start with the right or left quarter on your side and make adjacent and overlapping cuts down to the scored line. Start

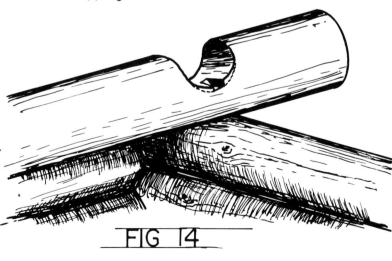

FIG 14

22

at the centre and work out. As the cut gets close to the scribed line, the wood will break cleanly away to the knife cut, and a clear boundary will easily be seen. This notch can be made very accurately in this manner, but if your skill with the saw will not permit this close an approach to the line, stay back about $\frac{1}{4}$" and finish with a chisel or a very sharp axe. When all 4 quarters have been shaped out, the finished notch is complete.

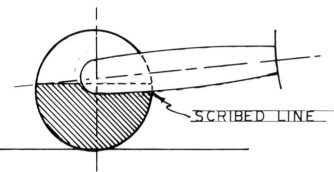

SCRIBED LINE

SECTION FIG 14

2

Photo #2 above shows the next cuts which remove most of the wood. Only 3 cuts are needed. Avoid the common error of making many cuts here, as if slicing a loaf of bread, as it accomplishes nothing except to make a smooth finish more difficult.

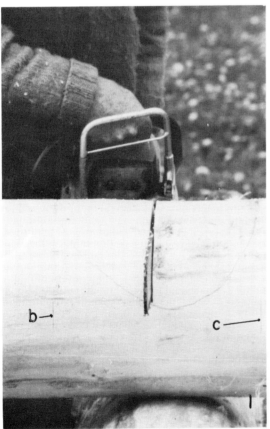

b →   c ——

Above, Photo #1, the initial cut in a rough notch. Note guide marks "b" - "c" and the cut line sketched in. At right, Photo #4, completed rough notch. Cut does not necessarily follow sketched line for rough notching.

3

Photo #3: overlapping cuts round out the notch.

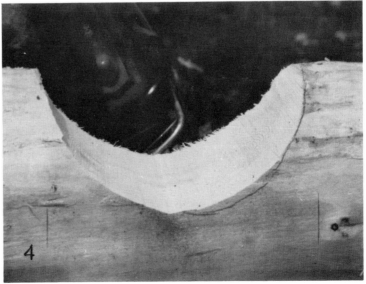

4

Lateral groove is a designation given to the cut which runs the length of a well-fitted log. There are a great many opinions as to how this groove should be cut and what the resulting section should look like.

In determining the best shape for this groove, we must first consider the effect of the cut on the material. Checking is caused by tension created in the outer layers of wood, generally the sapwood. Consequently the check will appear at the weakest point. The groove will almost always qualify as the weakest area and a crack will appear along its length. This tendency to localize checking to the bottom of the log is desirable. But if a large, wide Vee cut is made, the weakened material will then split and tend to spread (Fig. 1).

A narrow Vee cut or, better yet, a cove, will sit on top of the next log and as well as retaining its shape will do a better job of forming a tight seal (Fig. 2).

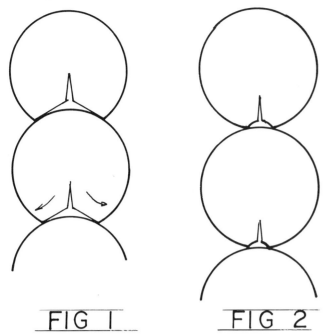

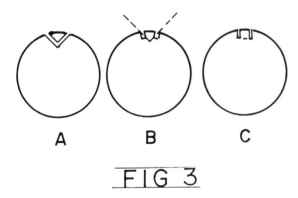

Vee grooves are most often cut with a chain saw although an axe or adze can do an excellent job.

There are at least three ways to cut the groove with a chain saw. In "A" (Fig. 3), the cuts are made inside the scribed line 1/8" to ½" depending on the size of the log. When the strip of wood has been removed, the cut is finished to the line by hand. A very sharp axe is essential for this, but various curved gouges, draw knives, and spoke shaves can also be of help.

Cutting the lateral groove may be done with the tip of the chain saw held at right angles to the work and the wood brushed out to the line by means of a careful sweeping motion. Good control is required here, in order to be accurate.

Most of the problems with fit are almost always interference or "hang-up" inside the scribed line (Fig. 4). Using a chain saw puts the operator far enough away from the work so that small lengths can be neglected -- and these are the skipped areas that will show up later to cause the hang-up problems. So check this work over well.

Another method which I like to use is to take a very shallow cut just inside each scribe line and on an angle near the radius of the log ("B", Fig. 3). Next make a second cut at an angle of about 45°. Use the width of the first cut as a hedge against overcutting the line while, at the same time, you can follow close to the line. If this is well done, there should be very little supplementary work required and the "Vee notch" will be kept flat enough to prevent excessive splitting while avoiding the danger of hang-up.

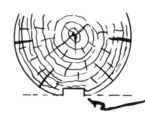

KEEP SCRIBE WIDTH NARROW AND COVE SIDES WELL TO AVOID HANG UP AT SIDES

A square groove ("C" Fig. 3) also has merit and holds insulation or moss very well. The drawback to this method is the tendency of many beginners to overcut and make far too wide and too deep a groove, as if making a dugout canoe. So this is a good groove only if this ancestral tendency is strictly avoided. The general rule is that the MAXIMUM WIDTH should be 1½" and the MAXIMUM DEPTH should be 1½". It is possible to cut this straight groove of uniform width the length of the log regardless of scribe width (Fig. 5).

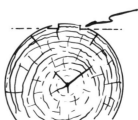

UPPER LOG IS SQUARE CUT AND FLATTENED TO THE SCRIBED LINE

LOWER LOG IS GROOVED DOWN TO SCRIBED LINE

When the groove has been cut, flatten the edges off with a plane or a slick, then work a groove along each scribe line on the lower log and leave a width of wood in the middle equal to the groove width in the upper log. Cut a little more (1/8") than the scribe depth. This will prevent the log length from accepting weight and, at the same time, provides a lock against the log shifting out of position. A precut strip of foam insulating material may be fitted into the groove. Some people have grooved both logs and put a plywood "feather" into this space. This is a bad building practice in that it tends to split the log

Above: Foam strip in place

and retains moisture in the lower groove. The foam material will tend to keep the log up and for this reason should be put in from the bottom after an additional round of logs has been fitted. This is done by jacking or wedging the logs up. Be sure to check the width and depth, however, before the log is finally turned down so that there will be no problem applying the foam later on.

If one does not care to use a chain saw, the lateral groove can be cut with either an axe or an adze. "Score" the log with an axe (Fig. 6). By cutting at an angle of about 45° across the log, the tip of the axe can enter the wood at the offside scribe line, and the swing should carry just enough momentum to allow the axe to continue to the near scribe line ("a" Fig. 6). At the last possible instant, the axe is allowed to overbalance so that the chip is flipped out.

The lateral groove is now almost complete and requires only "cleaning up" to finish it. With either a curved adze or an axe, work virtually across the grain of the log so that the final effect is a coved lateral groove ("b", Fig. 6).

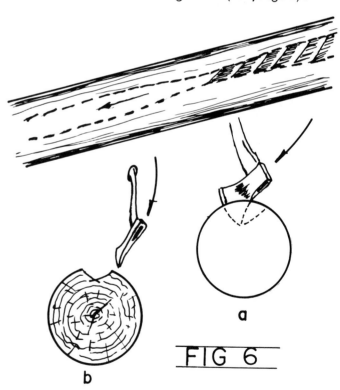

FIG 6

A good axeman can accomplish this work almost as quickly as can a man working with a chain saw. It requires a little greater effort but the rewards are many, not the least of which is the enjoyment of a more peaceful day.

SADDLE NOTCH

The round notch is often called a saddle notch and indeed the difference is not great. The use and application is about the same but the saddle notch is perhaps a little faster to do and therefore is often used for outbuildings and fences. The only reason it is sometimes shunned for use on a house is because the axe work shows. I am in sympathy with this viewpoint, but this is a characteristic shared with many other notches and is not important enough to cause a builder to discard it if it otherwise suits his purpose. This notch has a long and honourable history of service to furtrader, trapper, and settler. I am happy to include it here.

therefore not firm, place a block under each notch to stabilize the log. These blocks should be equal in height and long enough to extend all the way through the notch. Scribe the length of the log. This notch is useful when only an axe is to be used and a good fit may be obtained.

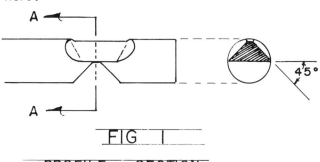

FIG I
PROFILE SECTION
OF SADDLE NOTCH

In practice, two flat surfaces, a and b (Fig.2), are cut at an angle of 45° to the vertical. These flats would nearly meet at the top of the log and should extend in length only as far as is required to accommodate the next log. The angle of the flat cuts may, at times, have to be modified to allow for logs that are of greatly differing size. Cut the top of the log down a little (c - Fig. 2) to give a flat surface of about 1" -- this will vary with the size of the logs.

The next log is brought into position and the width and depth of the notches marked on it. This may be accomplished as outlined in the section on "Round Notches". Many people, however, just cut the notch and rely on their judgment. This is a good way to develop an "eye" for size and distance.

Roll the log into place and scribe it. The notch may be scribed to a better fit at this time, if this is needed. If the notch is a good fit but the log touches the one below and is

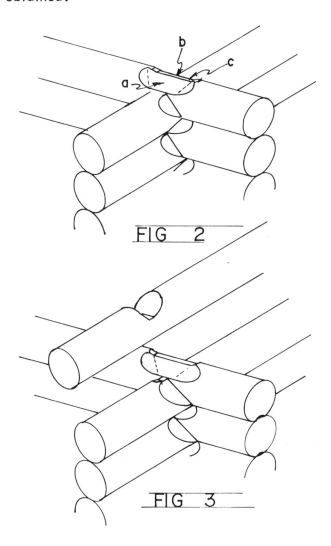

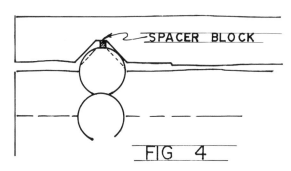

SQUARE NOTCH
(DOUBLE SCRIBED NOTCH)

This notch is not strictly a wall notch but may be found of good use in special applications. I am including it here because it is very good as a first log and last log notch. In these positions it is very firm and will not permit the logs to move or roll. It is also very good for purlins or corbels on the gable ends. Perhaps one of the best applications for a square notch is to handle a recurve situation as illustrated below (Fig. 1).

At this time, it is a good idea to scribe the full length of the log, although such a wide scribe may cause inaccuracy. Do each end. But before the log is moved, pick out and draw the level cuts (Figure 3). By using the same setting on the scribers, locate 4 points on each log, which will become the mated surfaces.

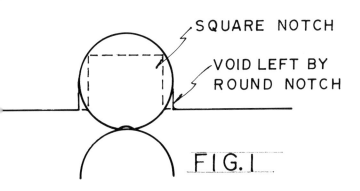

SQUARE NOTCH

VOID LEFT BY ROUND NOTCH

FIG. I

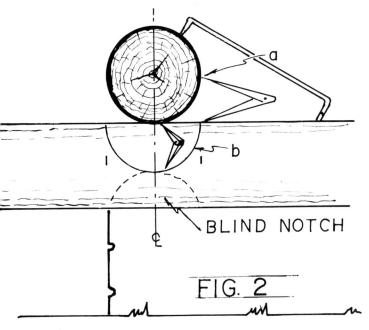

BLIND NOTCH

FIG. 2

In order to cut a square notch, the log to be fitted is placed in its final position, directly over the log below -- that is, with the bow of the log up, and centred on the wall (Figure 2).

FIG 3

Draw a level line a-a^1 (Fig. 3) to intersect the scribed line at a^1.

With the dividers at a^1 locate point b on the scribed line below. With the level, extend this point to b^1 and from b^1 locate point c. Carry on around the logs until you are back at point a.

If the layout has been done carefully, these points should match well.

Roll the log inward until the bottom side is up and join points a^1 - c and a - c^1 with straight lines around the circumference of the log (Fig. 4). Cut with a chain saw or a hand saw on these lines down to the scribed line and remove the wood. Do this for both logs.

29

From each line (a – a¹ etc.), cut down at right angles to the flat plane and cut to the scribed line. This is perhaps best done with a carpenter's chisel and mallet. I often rough this in with a small chain saw by holding it in a perpendicular position. The danger of kick-back is great, with this sort of cut, and caution is required.

When all 4 cuts have been made, check the measurements to be sure that the logs will fit, and you should obtain good results when the log is rolled down. Additional small scribes may be necessary the first few times and it will be more difficult to roll the log back up than for most notches. It is advisable to lift and block the log up a little, before attempting to roll it.

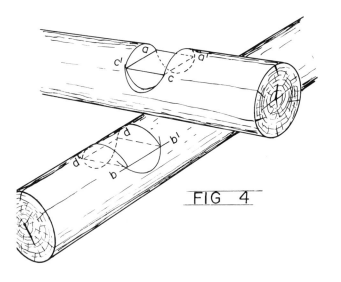

FIG 4

Photo #2. Nearby help keeps the log suspended long enough to show the interlocking positions of all the surfaces.

Photo #1. The Square Notch has been cut and is ready to be rolled down into position.

Photo #3. Final appearance of the notch: firmly interlocking without any loss of its natural log appearance.

Cuts $c - a^1$ and $c^1 - a$ may be spaced more closely. This may be done when it is desirable to place the upper log in a very low relative position. This might be for floor joists, ceiling joists, purlins, or other special conditions.

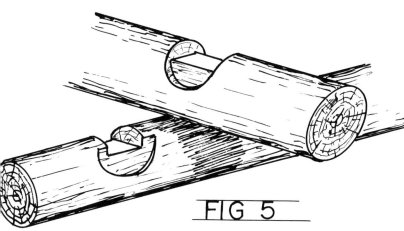

FIG 5

Fig. (5) illustrates the cuts used if one notch must be narrow -- in this case, the bottom log, although the same would apply to either log. This will handle most situations since the notch illustrated in Fig. (6) would most often be replaced with another notch. In cutting this notch, care must be taken to observe the difference in each log cut, otherwise a void will appear along the side.

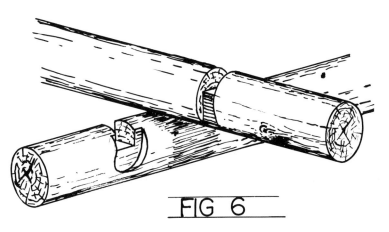

FIG 6

31

MITRED LAPPED NOTCH

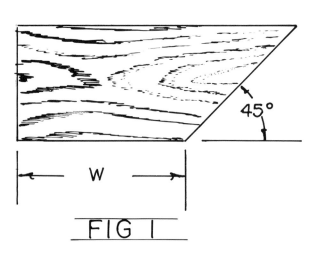

This notch is very simple in concept but a little more difficult to do. Because the side cuts are identical on every log, it lends itself to jig setups and even, perish the thought, to machining.

The mitred lapped notch is used for wall construction but finds its best use in detail work such as porch rails, verandah work, and other semi-structural positions. Because the side cuts are at 45° a template is useful. The size will depend upon the size of the logs.

45°

W

FIG 1

Figure 1 shows the shape of a plywood template which can readily be made to serve as a guide when cutting notches of this kind. If some sort of assistance is not used, the only way to obtain a good tight corner would be by trial and error. Such an approach is acceptable for one or two notches but time spent in making a template will pay dividends in speed as well as accuracy.

The sketch below shows the shape of the notch being worked on. The "square" piece left in the centre will always be the same length and the same width, but the height will vary with the size of the logs used and the amount of wood scribed out for the lateral groove. Keep the notch tight because the shrinkage of the log will tend to make all parts looser. This is not a shrink-fit notch and, for this reason, it is not the best wall notch.

The above photograph shows a mitered joint where the King Post and the Collar Tie cross. A mortise and tenon join would have served as well, but the visual effect would have been less striking.

The actual support is obtained by the two principal rafters, held in place with a collar tie. The arch formed by purlin and collar braces has little weight to accept here because of the large size of the purlins.

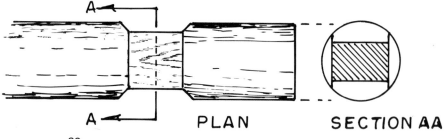

A

A

PLAN   SECTION AA

FIG 2

1

Photo #3, below. The finished notch. The side cuts are sloped but the cut, top and bottom, are square. All logs will be shaped the same.

Work may be done on the ground before the log is raised to the building. Keep the top and bottom cuts shallow; this can be corrected if need be when the log has been scribed. In order to scribe the log, place it in position over the wall. If one end has to be raised to level the log, place a spacer (a piece of wood) under the notch. Scribe the lateral groove in the usual way, then check the flats of the notch with the same scribe width. Cut to the scribe.

Photo #1. Start by cutting the side notch. The flat part "W" will be about one-half of the diameter of the average-sized log. The depth of the cut will therefore be about $\frac{1}{4}$ of the diameter if the logs are fairly uniform in size. If they are not, the cut will be deeper in the large ends and perhaps very shallow at the small end. In either case, the width "W" will remain the same and the slope of the sides will be 45°.

In the sample I am working on, in Photo #1, I am using a light axe to slope the sides. The cut was first made by cutting a steep "V" to the flat surface and taking out the wood with the adze, then finishing with a slick.

3

2

Photo #2. Check the slopes with a template to see that they are 45°. Keep the slope a little on the tight side so that any inaccuracy can be remedied later. Do both sides and the basic notch is complete. This same operation can be done with a chain saw, but use a small one. Make the first cuts straight down to the flat surface ("W"), split out the wood, then smooth with a gentle, sweeping motion.

33

4

A third log is now placed at right angles (Photo #5, lower left) and scribed to fit. The length of the log is scribed in the usual way -- that is, choose the widest space and adjust the scribers to that width or a little wider. At the notch, it is necessary to apply the same scribe height.

Photo #4 above is a bottom view of the notch as it would look from below. The first log that is being fashioned in Photo #1 was cut in half horizontally and placed on the "foundation". A second log with an identical notch was placed across the first notch. The flat surface "d" (Fig. 3) was cut to a depth which would permit this second log to come down to the foundation.

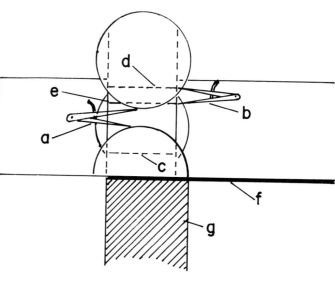

FIG 3

5

With the scribers set ("a", Fig. 3), place the lower point on the flat "e" and mark one corner of the upper flat "d" as shown by the scriber position "b". Do this on all 4 corners and when the points are joined, the flat to be cut is located. At times it is difficult to see the corners of flat "e". This problem is overcome by extending the lines of "e" onto the adjacent slope.

6

Photo #6, left, shows the appearance of the finished notch. When the newly completed notch is first assembled, it should be very tight because there is no real sealing off of these cuts and they would be dependent upon caulking for weatherproofing. The other drawback of this notch is the visibility of the cut surfaces. Not only is a portion of the square visible, but the 45° slope is also visible at the same level.

Photo #7, lower left, shows the fit of the lateral groove. The cove portion is of a slightly smaller radius than the lower log, in order to provide ventillation for the extended end and also provide a sharp edge for the scribe length -- this makes the fit close and accurate, but will not accept too much of the weight of the log. The greater proportion of the weight must be carried on the corners of the building.

Photo #8 shows the completed notch and lateral groove ready to be rolled into place.

8

7

SHEEP'S HEAD NOTCH

To introduce the sheep's head notch is to introduce, also, a whole group of notches designed to maintain their fit as the wood shrinks ... a "shrink-fit" notch.

The forerunner of these notches would undoubtedly have been the round notch and the saddle notch but the origins of all these are so much older than our written history, this can only be a matter of surmise.

This group of notches also carries a few colloquial names so, because this configuration has been in general use, I prefer to give it the descriptive name which is understood everywhere.

It has been, in the recent past, the practice of some ethnic groups to foster the misconception that they alone are capable of a particular expertise in log building. This of course is done in the economic hope that when such skills are required, their expertise will be the only ones sought. This practice in the particular instance of log buildings has tended to choke off new builders, and had almost succeeded in eradicating these skills from the 20th century. If, indeed, there has been a low ground rumble now and then in the British Isles, it is easily explained ... I am quite certain it occurs each time someone extinguishes my ancestry with the delighted exclamation, "Ah, you MUST be a Finn (or a Norwegian, or whatever the case may be in that locality) and your real name is undoubtedly spelled 'Maki' which means (fill in the blank) in Finn (or Norwegian, or whatever) ..." and in my mind's inner ear, I can hear the entire clan Mackay spinning in their graves in Scotland. For, in fact, were I to undertake to perpetuate myths, I believe I could do a very good job of it, as my studies in architectural history leave no doubt that I did indeed choose ancestors who were worthy timber builders. It was in the British Isles that timber building first reached its zenith and Julius Caesar's invading Romans -- great builders (in stone) that they certainly were -- felt they could do no finer than to copy, in wood, what the Anglo-Saxons were doing. The Norman invasion of England did little to change that pattern ... and between these two events came the invading Norsemen who LEARNED the art

of timber building there, for the first time and were then able to carry the knowledge back to their respective homelands. But for my part, I believe it would be a sorry day indeed if any young person in any part of this world could not say, "I, too, can build beautifully." And while there is no denying that some builders are extraordinarily gifted in the individual sense, I, as a teacher, am convinced that this trade is a learned skill ... and that anybody, of any nationality, can learn it. Therefore it is no coincidence in my mind, that the exposure of these myths (and certainly this includes the equally limiting "log cabin" myth) is largely responsible for the exploding resurgence of log construction on this continent today. Quality logwork is not the hereditary prerogative of any ethnic group ... which is to say, coming back to the sheep's head notch, that I prefer to call it by a name that is well understood by all log builders.

The sheep's head notch, like all others in horizontal log construction, leaves about one-half of the height of the log intact. It cuts away the other half because essentially there are twice as many logs at the corners as on the sides of the building. What is different about the sheep's head notch is that it attempts to prevent roll; they lock the log from displacement at the corner, and they tend to retain their fit as the log shrinks.

The round notch has been questioned, in this regard, because theoretically when the bottom log shrinks a loosening effect is possible at the sides (Figure 1). If the logs are well chosen and

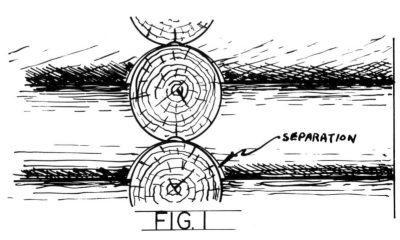

—SEPARATION

FIG. I

step, then, is a double cut which has the added advantage of helping to prevent end movement and twist (Figure 3).

Photo #1. This construction uses a round notch and despite the fact that the logs were freshly cut when placed on the building, no separation at the notch is apparent.

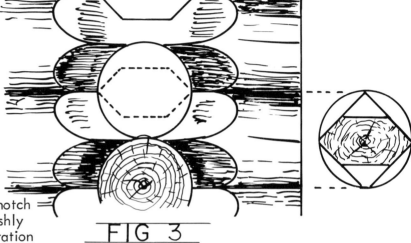

FIG 3

not notched below the diameter of its mate, this effect is inconsequential, even if green logs are used (Photo #1). But another solution is the saddle notch which, because the retained wood is cut at 45°, will maintain its fit when the wood shrinks (Figure 2). The next logical

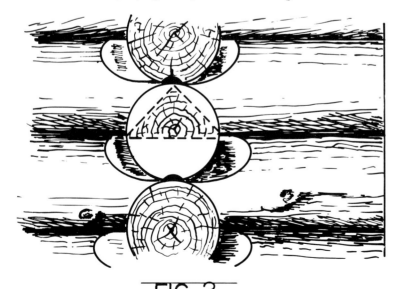

FIG. 2

It is good to note that all of these notches can be made easily with an axe and in some cases perhaps with an adze. The reason for this is that housed cuts would require a different kind of tool (chisels) and axes were undoubtedly the most ubiquitous of instruments.

With some additional effort, all of these notches can be constructed in such a manner that the axe cuts will not show. It is a matter of personal taste, really, which method is adopted.

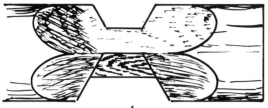

SHEEP'S HEAD

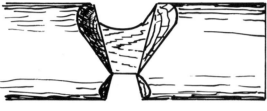

AXE HEAD

DIAMOND

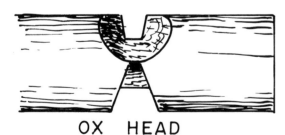

OX HEAD

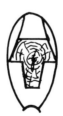

FIG 4

The variety of configurations found for this notch in Scandinavian countries is due, in part, to the logs having been shaped to cross-sectional shapes which are different than natural logs. The reasons why these shapes were undertaken would be a matter of speculations since the oldest of the buildings exhibiting these logs were built approx. A.D. 1300, some 300 years or more after the Viking raids on England had ceased, so that there is no direct record for these buildings. Three reasons are immediately apparent, however: One is that the sapwood of the tree is removed, or partly removed, and the life expectancy of the material is greatly increased. The ability of heartwood to resist decay was undoubtedly noted by these ancients since technology had not, by that time, separated men so far from their surroundings that such simple facts could go unnoticed. The second reason, where logs are split down the centre, would be to make better use of logs which were much larger than would be required for insulation even in a very immoderate climate and, at the same time, a flat interior wall would be provided. A third reason would be to obtain a finished appearance for the building, a medium through which an experienced builder could demonstrate his skill.

A sheep's head notch therefore will work with a round log and is, in fact, quite easy to shape. However, an elongated log would require an elongated version of the same notch ... which is the oxhead notch.

Some of the shapes and resulting notches are illustrated in Figure 4.

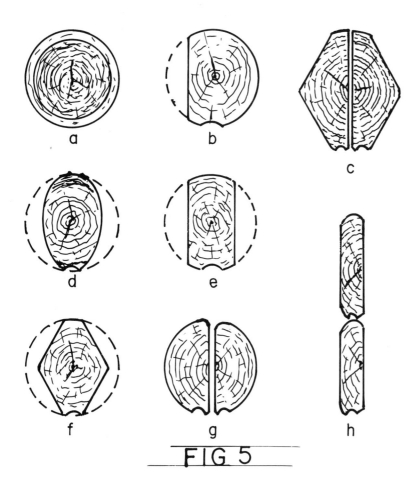

FIG 5

Figure 6 illustrates how a ring of a particular shape might be slid over a log to acquire a uniform shape.

The same sort of thing has been done with machinery but the results leave much to be desired.

In the first place, the logs described here were large and produced spectacular results, as compared to the poles being subjected to the machines of today.

In the second place, these logs were produced by craftsmen who placed value on their skill. Each log became a work of art; each house a monument.

Figure 5 shows a variety of log shapes which might be found in early buildings. "a" is a round log with the sapwood represented by the lighter outside ring. In "b" the sapwood has been hewn off one side. And in "e" both exposed sides are hewn but the top and bottom are untouched except for fitting. The log in "c" has been slabbed off to a diamond shape, then split down the centre; this provides a log shape on the exterior and a flat surface on the interior, while the work involved is not too great. Shape "d" has been formed from a rough hewn log by sliding a ring over the log and removing any wood which interferes. Again the sapwood has been removed but the height of the log is not diminished. Logs "f" and "g" are similar to "c" and "h" and would more properly be called plank construction.

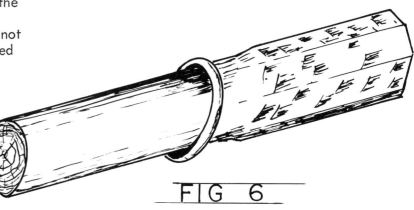

FIG 6

To construct the sheep's head notch, first cut a narrow notch about $\frac{1}{4}$ of the log diameter in depth (Photo #2).

The sides should slope at 30° and the width should be no greater than will permit a shoulder when this slope reaches the diameter of the next log (Figure 7).

This notch will be the same width and depth as the lower half ("c") of the cross section in Figure 7.

2

Photo #2, above. First cut of a sheep's head notch.

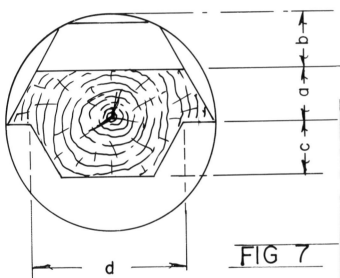

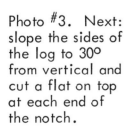

FIG 7

3

Photo #3. Next: slope the sides of the log to 30° from vertical and cut a flat on top at each end of the notch.

Photo #5, below. The first cut has been made in the upper log.

The cut originates at the width marks and proceeds to a depth equal to "a" (Fig. 7).

The sides of the cut should slope at 30°. It is a good idea to start by sloping these cuts more -- say, 40°, and then work them in at the bottom to the correct angle, with a template for a guide.

Sketch the width of the notch in the lower log "A", onto the upper log, then extend the sloped cuts (on the upper log) down to "B". The width at this point should be the same as "B" on the lower log and the depth should be equal to "b" in Figure 7. At this time extend the

Photo #4, above. Place the next log across the building and as near the notch as possible. Mark the width of the lower log on the log to be fitted.

Accuracy is required here because if the notches are, for instance, too far apart, then one or both of them will have to be enlarged. This will not only occasion momentary frustration but will also produce a draughty notch. Avoid this problem by placing a centre mark at each end of the log to be cut and checking the centres' measurement of the receiving log.

"a", Photo #4, points out width measurements; "b" points out centres' measurement locations.

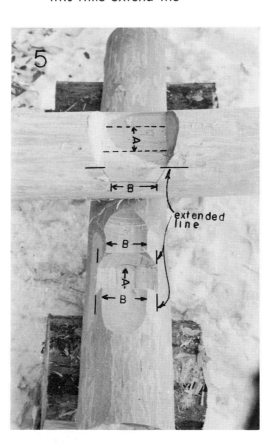

lines of the flat surfaces onto the sides of the logs adjacent (as applied on Photo #5). These will be handy references when the log is rolled into position, both to check that the flats fit well together (as the marks should then co-incide) and to use as a reference point if the log must be scribed down farther.

Photo #6, above. The final cut has been made.

This cut can be roughed in with an axe, then finished with an adze or a chisel and mallet. On this cut, I used an axe and finished with a slick.

Remember that the internal slope is also at 30°. The accuracy of the slope can be checked with a template such as is illustrated in Figure 8.

42

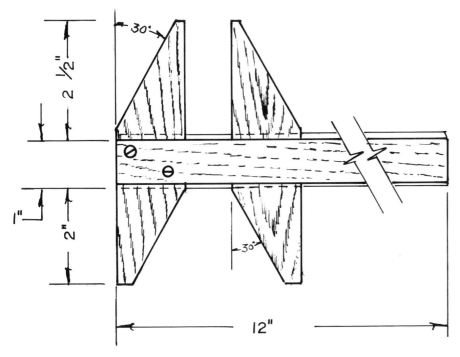

8

ADJUSTABLE TEMPLATE FOR USE
WITH SHEEPS HEAD NOTCHES
FIG 8

Photo #8, above. The log that has just been placed is now ready for the next log.

It is necessary to have had this next log chosen before this point is reached, because these notches are not of uniform size. The slope of the sides remains the same but the width and depth may vary as the butts and the tops are interchanged at the corners.

As in all horizontal log construction you should try to intersect the corners at the diameter point of the logs. This may not always be possible with a limited choice of logs, but the work is much better if this can be accomplished, and a sheep's head notch, like any other, is then simpler to fit.

Photo #7, lower right. The completed notch is in place. This notch is very easy to make and has good weather resistance. The sloped sides are intended to maintain a fit when the log shrinks although the arbitrary 30° is a compromise, in order to make all the slopes the same. If winter-cut or reasonably dry logs are used, the notch will remain tight. The notch has good support characteristics and resists roll if most of the weight is carried at the corner. One feature of this sheep's head notch is that it can be made with an axe and consequently reduces the use of a chain saw around the building. The only objection I make, to this notch, is that the axe cuts remain visible but because they are the manifestation of honest work (and if the cuts are kept to a uniform length) they soon become **inconspicuous** as the building ages.

ROUND SHEEP'S HEAD

●●●●●●●●●●●●●●●●●●●●●●●●●●●●●●●●●●●●●●●

This notch is keyed against movement either laterally or sideways and, because it has a tongue and groove all the way around, it is very weathertight. It is a more difficult notch to fit and will require scribers with an accurate level, as well as the use of a template, in order to attain production speed. By production speed, I mean the kind of progress whereby an individual must place 4 logs a day if he's to get the building up within a reasonable length of time. And by a reasonable length of time, I am using those terms of reference imposed by wind and weather upon the building materials, plus a respectful acknowledgement of the too-swift passing of one's days upon earth. It is well worth noting that any builder capable of a good steady pace is most often doing a superior quality of work. The efficient use of tools seems to result in the equally efficient use of time.

When your next log has been selected and placed on the building, cut the bottom notch with reference to this log (Figure 9).

Line "a" – "b" may be laid out with a level, but the line should extend well beyond the notch for future use (Photo #9).

Slope the sides to 30° from the vertical. This may be cut with either an axe or a chainsaw. At first it might be a wise precaution to cut straight down to the width "B", Figure 9, then

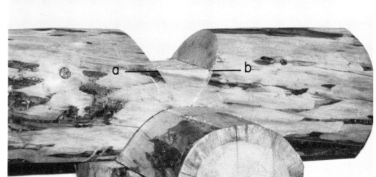

9

slope the sides afterward with an axe or a chisel. Continue the slope at 30° on down to the log below (Photo #9); however, this weather seal is also sloped at 30°. This is no problem because it will be harmonious with the angle of the side of the log. It may also be checked with the template (Figure 10).

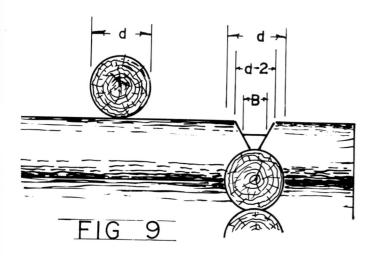

FIG 9

The notch should be about $\frac{1}{4}$ of the log diameter in depth, ideally, or $\frac{1}{2}$ of the exposed wood (Photo #9). However, each situation is a little different and this may be adjusted accordingly.

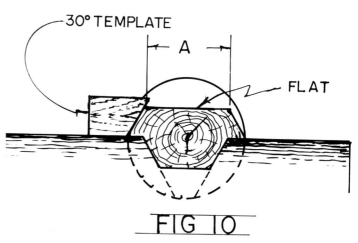

FIG 10

Roll your new log into the notches now formed. If required, block one end or the other up, in order to obtain a uniform scribe from end to end. Use your dividers with line "a" – "b" as a base, place points "c" and "d" on the new log at a distance equal to the width of your scribe (Photo #10).

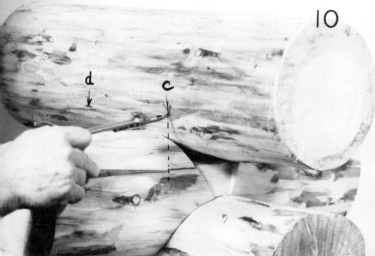

3/4" carpenter's chisel to do the one shown in these photographs, but on other occasions I have done this round sheep's head notch with a small chain saw. So use whichever implement you feel confident with.

These steps should be performed on each side, and each end, of the log; and when points "c" and "d" are joined, you will have established the plane for the flat surface of this notch.

With the same scriber setting, scribe the remainder of the notch (Photo #11) and the length of the log in the normal way.

Photo #13, above, shows the final notch. The key piece at the ends of the notch form an excellent weather seal. Note the square cut of the lateral groove on the near end of the log. (Refer to section on LATERAL GROOVES for an explanation of this.) Photo #14, below, shows the appearance of the completed round sheep's head notch.

Roll the log back up (always, for safety's sake, toward the inside of the building) and cut a square-sided notch of a length "A" equal to the width "A" of the log below.

Draw in width "B" equal to length "B" of the log below, and sketch in the end slope at 30°. The round part of the notch may now be cut. I used a

LOG END TREATMENT

Round log construction and much hewn log construction embodies an overhang or extension of the log beyond the building. This overhang is a part of the notch, and it is essential for stability of the wall. It locks the logs in place and assists in preventing roll. Therefore, a few rules are needed to ensure the quality of the structure; but beyond that, how the log ends are cut or shaped is largely a matter of personal preference.

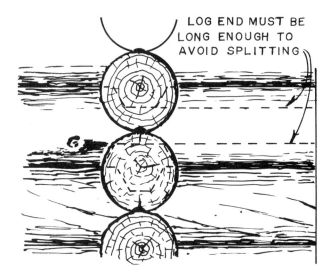

LOG END MUST BE LONG ENOUGH TO AVOID SPLITTING

Fig. 1. Ensure that the end beyond any notch is long enough that the keying will not split off.

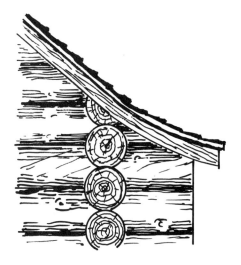

Fig. 2. Protect the overhang from weather. The roof must extend far enough to cover the log ends ends and keep them dry.

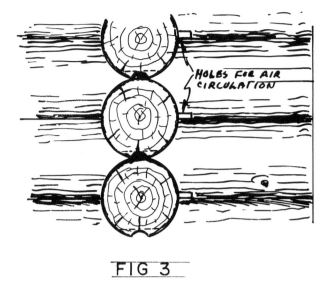

FIG 3

Fig. 3. Arrange for ventillation. Where the logs are too tightly together, any water in the form of rain or snow blown onto the logs, or even high air humidity, may leave the logs in a moist state for lengthy periods and this is always a preparation for decay.

Fig. 4 below shows an opened end for use where moisture conditions are extreme.

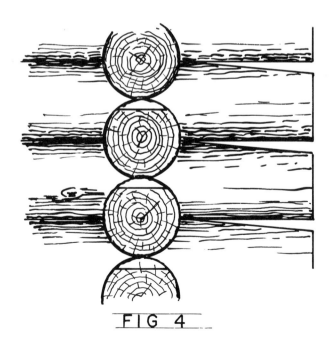

FIG 4

The profile of the end cut, to a degree, sets the the tone of the building. If the log ends are flared wide at the bottom, the effect becomes that of a very solid, heavy building. A flaring outward at the top gives an impression of lift and lightness to the building (Figure 5).

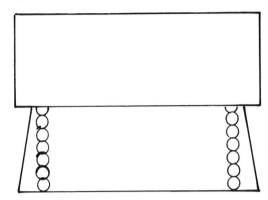

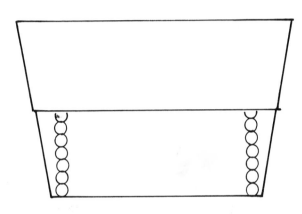

FIG 5

These slopes may be used in combination, as well, to locate the visual weight as desired (Fig. 6).

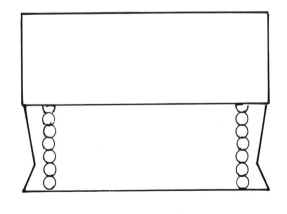

FIG 6

Log ends cut vertically give a more formal appearance to the house, while ends cut short set a more severe tone (Fig. 7). Staggered ends are considered to be less formal in appearance, to the point of being rustic.

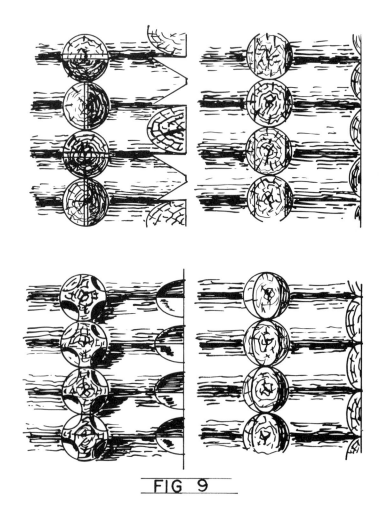

FIG 7

The additional work done on the log ends will not materially change the quality of the work but will greatly enhance the general impressions of the building. One of the most readily executed bits of artistry of this nature is a slight bevelling around the circumference of the log ends (Fig. 8). Other possibilities are illustrated in Figure 9.

These several configurations illustrated in Figure 9 do not, by any means, exhaust the possibilities open to the designer or builder. As in most aspects of log building, the imagination of the designer is the only limiting factor. In truth, it could well be argued that the designer-builder has not yet picked up the challenge which is before him.

FIG 9

When log ends are corbeled out (to borrow a term from brick layers and stonemasons (see "a", Fig. 10), care should be taken to locate the precise end of the log and scribe that length to the log above so that the lateral groove may end at that spot. Photo #3, opposite page, is a good example of this need having been taken into account.

48

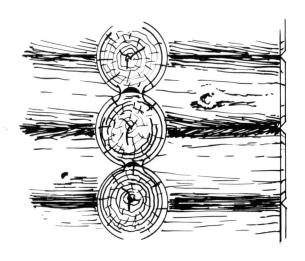

FIG 8

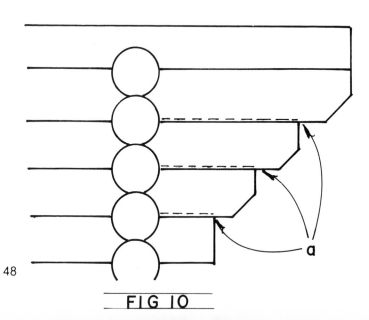

FIG 10

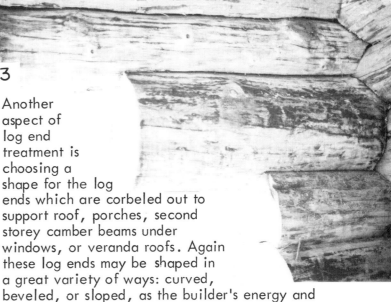

3

Another aspect of log end treatment is choosing a shape for the log ends which are corbeled out to support roof, porches, second storey camber beams under windows, or veranda roofs. Again these log ends may be shaped in a great variety of ways: curved, beveled, or sloped, as the builder's energy and imagination directs. One aspect of this which has not, to my knowledge, yet been investigated is the carving of these ends to represent salient aspects of our culture. Perhaps there are no salient aspects to our culture that lend themselves to patient carving.

Photo #1, upper left, is shown here to illustrate an error which can hinder making a good appearance of the log ends. The lateral groove has been extended as a "V" cut much too close to the end so that trimming the log ends has exposed the "V", leaving a somewhat inexpert appearance. For this reason, I try to encourage anyone who cuts a "V" groove not to extend the "V" past the wall notch -- but to use a cove all the way, in case of any change of plan which would require a shortening of the logs.

Photo #2, below left, shows a different shape on a building under construction. Here the logs are scooped flat from the diameter of one down to the diameter of the next. A similar shape is used in reverse order at the top of the wall.

In the scurry to bring a building to completion, this aspect of finishing has been (often through necessity) neglected or put off to a later date. It is certainly a thing which can be undertaken at any time; and perhaps that time should be much later, when the sawdust has settled, and the builder is sufficiently recovered to approach the final touches with a more artistic outlook.

NOTCHES FOR HEWN TIMBER

DOVETAIL

For the purposes of organization of this study, the wall notches have been separated into two groups: those used on round logs and those used on hewn logs.

Often, in practice, the two groups are interchanged and we find a notch, described here as belonging to hewn timber, used on round logs. Certainly, almost any notch is interchangeable; however, the basis of selection is the probable historic origin of each. A dovetail notch can be used on almost-round timber but at least one side must first be hewn for a short distance, and the top and bottom of the notch are hewn surfaces. It therefore seems logical to assume that the dovetail notch was developed to join hewn timbers. Too, I think a dovetail corner looks better on hewn logs, although I have seen some very nice examples in round log construction.

There is also a considerable similarity between notches used on round, as compared with square, timbers. For instance, a mitered notch is very much like a lapped notch. But because the rounds are left on, the manner of construction may vary. A sheep's head notch is essentially the same as an oxhead notch, the latter being simply elongated to accommodate the different cross section of the hewn material.

Above: hewn logs with saddle notch. Note breakdown caused by close-cut ends (ref. LOG END TREATMENT).

Below: hewn logs with lapped notch.

Above. Round log house with dovetail corners.

Therefore the notches selected for description under hewn timber may well be used (in some cases) on round logs. The choice is largely arbitrary, and for discussion purposes, since the origins of most have long since disappeared into the mists of antiquity.

The first notch in this group must be the dovetail notch. Almost everyone concerned with timber building is familiar with the general form of this join, even if he has not so far possessed himself of the details of construction. Too often, people are intimidated by the folklore of this skill and speak of a dovetail notch with awe and wonder. "You couldn't slip a knifeblade between the joins anywhere" is the common compliment and the builder is accorded a high degree of reverence for his skills. It really is not at all difficult to achieve.

Above. Dovetail work in Alberta. Photo by Rae McIntyre, Carrot Creek, Alberta.

applies to all types of notches in a greater or lesser degree, so it is a bridge that must be crossed in all cases.

Dovetail notches have been used almost exclusively for the construction of permanent buildings. Houses and outbuildings that were a major undertaking of a careful builder will exhibit a wide spectrum of skill with this notch. It is a strong and durable notch, and it can also be an important factor if the timber is a bit on the short side since there is no extension of the corner. Of all the older buildings still standing across Canada, the majority, I'd guess, would have dovetail corners. It is difficult to determine whether this is because of a greater ability to withstand the wear of time, or whether the builders who were capable simply preferred to use a dovetail corner. In any event, this notch appears to have the greatest lifespan and be more able to maintain itself without a roof, even, than any other notch. Houses are still built in this way (see photo below) but I have not seen any modern new homes in hewn log construction.

Above. New log work with dovetail corners. This example was done at the B. Allan Mackie School of Log Building by students who had no previous experience in logwork.

The dovetail is perhaps less difficult to make than a round notch. The only area where a little more skill may be needed could be in the selection of logs. If you are not a good judge of logs, you could get into trouble by putting the wrong one in any given place on a building. As each round progresses, the next pair of logs must be somewhat higher than the last pair, but not so much higher that the following pair will be unable to cover the ends. But this same rule

Suitable timber, skill, and determination, seem to have vanished in that order. I have great hopes, however, that they will soon be redis-covered in the reverse order. I think the first two steps of such a process have already been taken so that I have some confidence that the last will surely follow -- and good timber will again be made available to builders.

The model building used here to illustrate several of these notches has the first $\frac{1}{2}$ log, which would rest on the foundation, dovetailed into the sill logs (Fig. 1). The procedure for this is shown in Photos #1, #2, and #3. This will avoid the appearance of $\frac{1}{2}$ logs extending over the foundation on the types of corners which have such an extension. For an ordinary dovetail corner, the first $\frac{1}{2}$ log may be treated as in the following description.

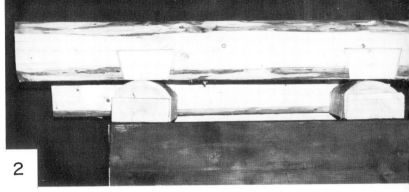

2

Photo #2. Sill log has been recessed to fit over the dovetail end of the first $\frac{1}{2}$ log.

3

Photo #3. Sill logs in place.

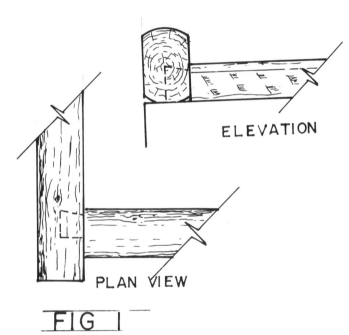

ELEVATION

PLAN VIEW

FIG 1

With the $\frac{1}{2}$ log and sill logs in place, the pro-cedure is as follows: all logs or log ends are hewn to an identical width, and the outside corner will be the point of reference ("a", Fig. 2).

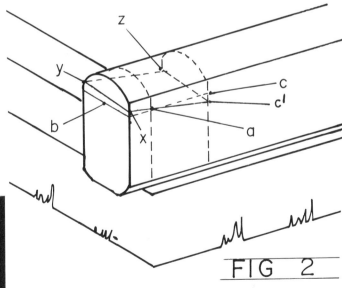

FIG 2

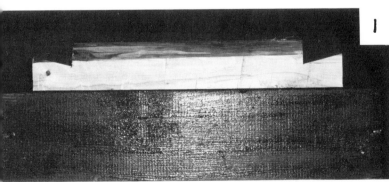

Photo #1. First $\frac{1}{2}$ log with dovetail key extending only halfway across foundation wall.

With a tape measure, locate a point "b", Fig. 2, approximately $\frac{1}{4}$ of the log diameter down from the top (Photo #4). Extend this point around the side to line "a". This allows

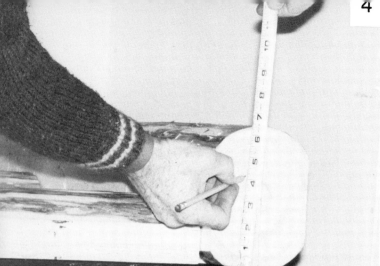

Photo #4, above. Measure down approx. $\frac{1}{4}$ of the log diameter.

Photo #6, above. "Draw a vertical line corresponding to the log width you have chosen"

Photo #5, below. Extend all 4 lines up (see also Photo #9).

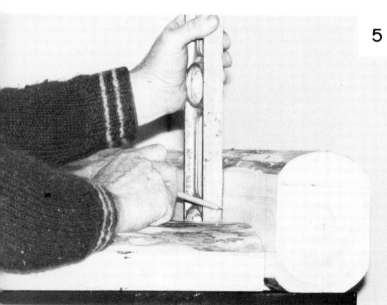

The $\frac{1}{2}$" measurement for slope is not an absolute. This can indeed be different for each log, but a reasonable uniformity is desirable and a slope of $\frac{1}{2}$" in 6" is efficient.

From point "x", place a level line across the end end of the log and from this line measure up the same distance ($\frac{1}{2}$") as before (call this point "y". Draw line "x" - "y". From point "y", measure back on the offside the width of the log and place a level mark on this line. Measure down the $\frac{1}{2}$" and draw "y" - "z" through this point (offside of log, Fig. 2) and extend the line to the vertical cut line (Photo #7). You have now established a sloped flat plane which will form the dovetail.

for a 2" or 3" extension of the log end for later trimming. Draw vertical lines up at all 4 locations on the notch for future use (Photo #5).

Continue this level line to point "c" (Fig. 2) on a vertical line corresponding to the log width you have chosen beyond line "a" (Photo #6). Locate "c¹" about $\frac{1}{2}$" below point "c" (Fig. 2) and with a straight edge (carpenter's level) join point "c¹" to point "a" and continue this line to the outside corner of the log (point "x", Fig. 2).

Photo #7, above. Extend point "y" through "z" on the vertical cut line.

Make the vertical cut with a handsaw (Photo #8) or a crosscut saw ... a chain saw is often too rough ... and shave off the wood to the line with a sharp axe or a large wood chisel. Do this on each end of the building, and you are ready for your next log (Photo #9).

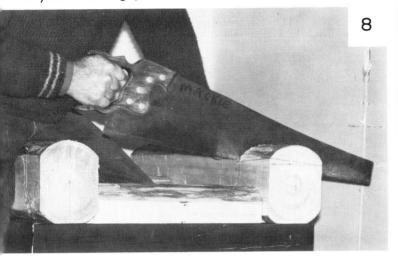

8

Photo #8, above. The vertical cut is best made with a hand saw.

9

Photo #9, above. The two log ends, ready for the next log.

Place the next log across the log ends already formed, in a position directly above the wall and relative in every other respect to the position it will finally occupy. A centre line drawn on the ends of the logs can be of assistance here, lining each log up with the previous line drawn. Next draw vertical lines up from each corner (a, b, c, d, Photo #10).

Choose your scribe setting and scribe the cut (Photo #10).This may be done by picking out points on lines a, b, c, d at the scribe distances above corresponding points on the lower flat surface and join them with a straight edge later.

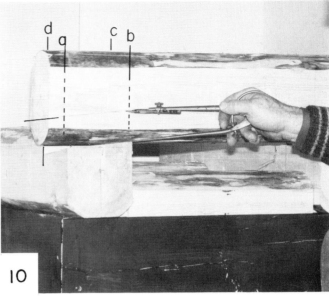

10

Photo #10, above. Scribe the next log to fit the prepared seat.

Scribe the length of the log at this time. Turn the log over and if an accurate cut is made to the scribed lines, a good fit should be obtained the first try (Photo #11). If the scribe distance is too great, it is quite acceptable to make a "rough" cut first to remove some of the wood and lower the log to a desirable height.

The dovetail is now complete (ref. BUILDING WITH LOGS for additional information) and it remains only to repeat the process in order to fit the next log. If your measurements were taken with care, you will not be surprised if an awed visitor exclaims that he is unable to slip a razor blade between the perfect surfaces of your dovetail notch ... although that sort of tightness is more often the characteristic of an aged building which has been subjected to the unrelenting pressures of tons and time.

Photo #11, below. Completed dovetail notch.

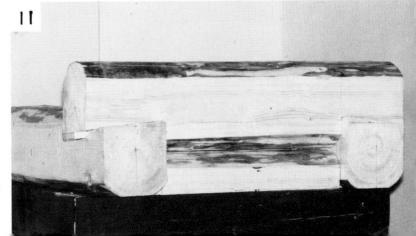

11

LOCKED DOVETAIL

Photo #11, left side, shows the additional feature of a locked dovetail. This would seem a most unnecessary precaution when a dovetail notch is in itself a locking device. However, time is a harsh overlord and anything which may extend useful lifespan is worthy of a builder's consideration. Some houses are built with this locked configuration on each notch. But most employ it only at the plate and sill. It is, in fact, not difficult to do and serves two purposes: (1) the completed log will retain its position very securely while the next log is being placed; this can be a problem in building otherwise, and the only other way to resolve it is recourse to spikes and pegs. (2) the lock notch will prevent logs moving out of the wall even with long use or abuse.

Sometimes houses were constructed with dovetail on only half of the notch (Photo #12). While this is sound construction, it does allow some logs to become displaced. This can happen for one of several reasons.

In all log construction, the greater proportion of the weight of the wall should rest on the corners, that is 70 to 80%. If this is not the circumstance, the greater weight between the corners tends to move the log either in or out of the wall, with an already-loosened corner to make this even more possible. The result will be a draughty corner because the joint has become loose, and insulation driven into this space further tends to dislodge the log.

56

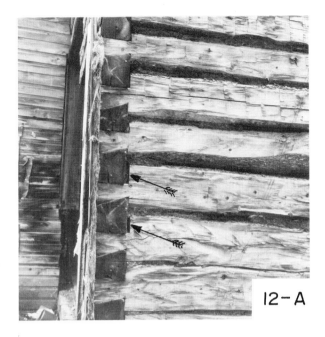

12-A

12-B

I am reminded of the story told to me by a dear friend, now retired, as to how he lost the first job he ever had, as a youth. The job was to drive a team of horses on a wagon (bundle rack) in northern Alberta in 1920. At lunch time it was required to bring the teams into the house-yard which had a driveway circling the house. My friend simply dropped his reins and jumped off the wagon close to the gate. The team ran away. Around the house they went, their eyes wide and nostrils flaring, and the bundle wagon cutting the corner and taking 3 logs out of the wall of the farmer's new house. It might have been pointed out to the farmer that, had the corners been full dovetail instead of lap joint, no damage would have been done ... but this apparently did not come up in the conversation that day. It was not until some years later that my friend reached this conclusion on his own.

The depth of the locking spline will depend on the size of the log. I do not think it would ever be advisable to make it more than 1" in depth. Generally $\frac{1}{2}$" to 3/4" is sufficient. Lay out the bottom half of the notch in the usual way, as described. When this is complete, lay out the lock as shown in Figure 3.

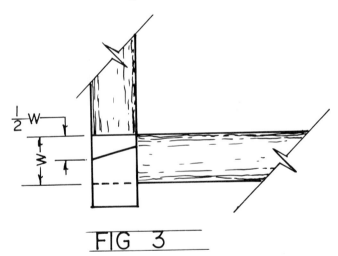

FIG 3

Photo #12, above. Two buildings in near proximity and of similar age.
12-A. $\frac{1}{2}$ dovetail with sloped cut on the top of the log and a level cut on the bottom. Shows displacement of the logs (arrows).
12-B. Full dovetail shows no separation. There are many instances when the $\frac{1}{2}$ dovetail retains its position but the full dovetail appears to be more stable.

The tapered slot may be cut with a handsaw and the wood removed with a chisel. The upper half of the notch may be scribed as for an ordinary dovetail. Take care to define the points where the lock is located. To begin with, it may be wise to draw a second line on the underside of the notch at a reduced height equal to the thickness of the lock (Fig. 4).

First cut to the lower line drawn (2nd line in Figure 4). Draw the key portion on the flat produced thereby and then cut to the original scribe for the part of the notch which must be lowered the additional $\frac{1}{2}$ to 3/4".

SCRIBE LINE
INITIAL CUT

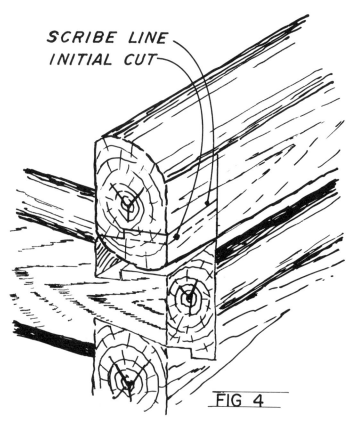

FIG 4

When the lateral groove, which was drawn at
the same time, is complete, the log is ready to
be put down. There is some satisfaction in
making this notch so tight that there is no movement possible in any direction except straight
up. The work is very secure as you progress. If
you should have any difficulty in making the
key fit, it is possible to fashion a gauge to
check the fit (Fig. 5). This sort of gauge is
useful for many kinds of joins and can be
quickly made to suit the project at hand.

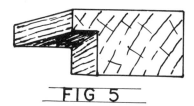

FIG 5

Houses of hewn logs are not rare in Canada.
Many of the "pioneer villages" have good
examples of these buildings and many such
buildings are still lived in, as they have been
for the past 100 years. I expect before long to
see new buildings of hewn log -- as soon as
able builders get the inspiration. I have noted
among my students that the "bug" for hewing
becomes an obsession; hewn log houses could
well be the result. Today's society is much
inclined to harrass its members for "progress"
and instant rewards. No one is willing to

devote several years to any project with this sort of a whipping going on. But in the early years of this country, people understood that it takes a good length of time to build a proper house. An oldtime broad axe man, Harry Osychuk, tells me that where he grew up in Alberta and Saskatchewan, they customarily took 6 years to build such a house. The logs were cut, hewn, and carefully piled to season for 3 years. Then the walls were erected and again left for 3 years to settle, before the finishing work could begin. As Harry -- one of the best axemen I have ever seen -- explains it, this length of time was not necessary for either the cutting, the seasoning, or the settling ... but rather, to obtain the few required dollars with which to purchase the finishing materials.

LOCKED OR BOXED LAP

Above. Hewn log building with lapped corners, locked with a corner extension. Ontario.

Lapped notches have been used extensively where time, and perhaps talent, have been in short supply. If the builder is capable of obtaining a scribed fit, however, he is readily capable of doing a dovetail notch -- which is just as quickly achieved as a lapped notch, and is infinitely superior.

However, the lapped notch may be used with confidence if there is an extension on the end of the log (Photo #1). The extension should be long enough that there is no danger of it splitting off during construction or afterward as the logs dry. 6" would be minimal.

The logs or log ends are hewn to a uniform width and two saw cuts, approx. $\frac{1}{4}$ of the log diameter in depth and the width of the next log, are made in the top of the log. The wood may be split out but work from both sides to avoid slabbing the offside. Rough the cut in with an adze or axe. Finish with a chisel or by brushing with a chain saw. This is very quick to do and the top half of the notch (in the next log) is equally quick and simple (Photo #2). The problem here is that shrinkage of the log will cause a loosening of the notch, with a resulting instability.

2

Photo #2, above. 2nd log: the cut is identical to first cut, except for suitable depth.

I

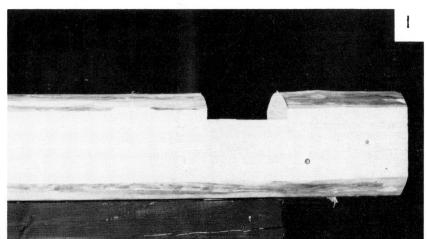

Photo #1, lower left. First cut for a boxed lap join.

Large buildings have been constructed with this notch. But I cannot recommend it for horizontal log building at all. There are so many other notches better suited to this job that this lapped notch should be considered only for framing.

A full lapped notch is similar in most respects to this lapped or boxed notch. The initial cuts are made about halfway through (Fig. 2). The extension portion of this notch is inclined to split off more easily or if no extension is built the notch must be spiked or dowelled to maintain it in position ... and for all these reasons it is a notch unworthy of the serious builder. It is now used only in those monstrosities of buildings that employ logs sawn on 2, 3, or even 4 sides (as in Figure 2).

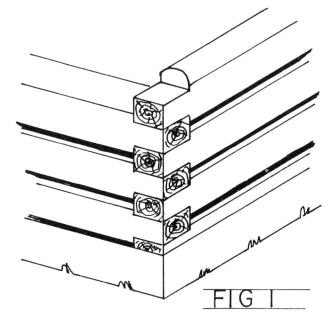

FIG 1

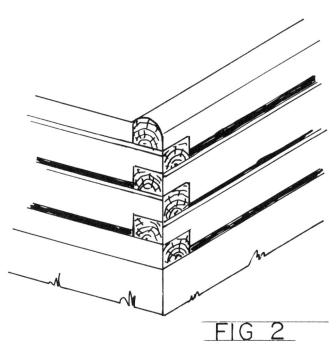

FIG 2

Figure 1. Common lapped joint.

Figure 2. Full lapped joint.

62

LOCKED LAP

A locked lapped notch is a different proposition altogether. It will retain its position very securely if well fitted. It will develop a small space ("a", Fig. 3) when the logs finally shrink and in this respect it is similar to a half-dovetail. (In a full dovetail, the logs tend to creep inward and therefore to tighten up.) This locked lapped notch can also be cut fully down so that the courses are level on top (Fig. 4) and for this reason I have used it for plate members in pièce-en-pièce construction.

This notch when used with an extended end ("b" Fig. 4) is very stable.

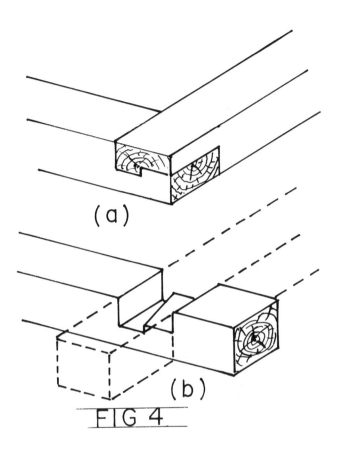

(a)

(b)

FIG 4

Figure 4, above, shows a fully lapped locked joint for use in plate construction.

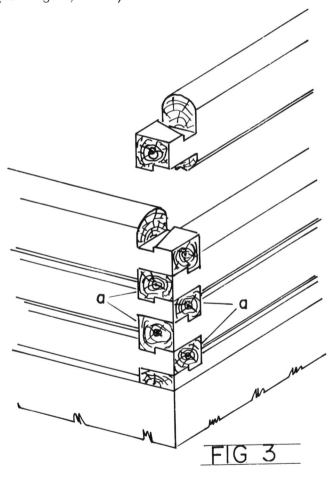

FIG 3

Figure 3, above, shows a locked lapped joint in wall construction.

OXHEAD NOTCH

●●

The oxhead notch is identical to a sheep's head notch with the exception that it is elongated to accommodate the hewn timber, or shaped timber as the case may be (see Page 39). This notch will remain tight and shed water well ... and for these reason it is greatly superior to lapped notches. It is also very stable in that it resists roll and warp in the timber. If the configuration is a bit confusing at first, be assured that this will clear up in the making of a practice notch. If a template is used to control the shape of the cuts, the notch is about as easy and as fast to make as any other. This type of notch is dependent upon an extension to the end of the log. A building of this style can be a beautiful thing, especially if larger logs are used and if particular attention is given to the embellishment of the log ends. The entire building can become a work of art.

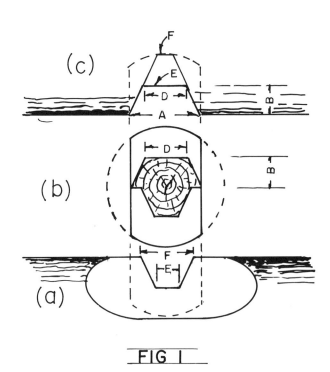

FIG I

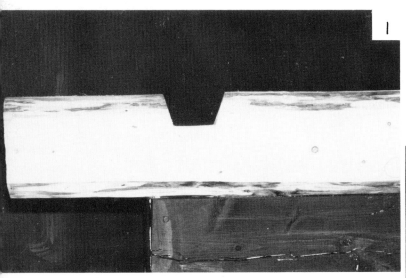

Photo #1, above. First cut for oxhead slope may become less than 30° as the width of the log in relation to height becomes less.

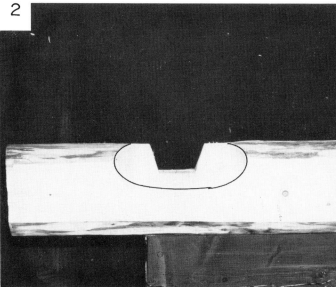

Photo #2. Side slope is cut on the lower log.

The initial notch, centred on the wall (Photo #1), is cut to a depth of about ¼ of the log diameter. The sides are sloped about 30°. The notch should be 1" to 1½" narrower than the log which will be placed on it. The sides of this log are then sloped from a point short of the centre down to the horizontal diameter line and again the slope should be near 30° (Photos #2 and #3) and ("a", Fig. 1).

Photo #3. Lower notch as it looks when finished.

This initial shaping may be done off the building but be very sure that the notches are the correct distance apart.

In order to scribe the log, place it in position with the centres carefully lined up vertically. Be sure that each end of the log is at similar heights. One end of the other may have to be blocked up to accomplish this. The length of the log may now be scribed, and the same scribe setting carried over the notch to take care of any small discrepancy that may exist. Cut away the excess wood and the fit should be similar to the notch in Photo #4.

3

The next log may be placed on the building or rough notched on the ground. Start the notch by using the width of the lower log (A, Fig. 1). Slope the sides of the notch at 30° and cut to a depth equal to "B", Fig. 1. Measurement "D" should now be nearly the same on each log. Mark length "E" as derived from the lower log ("a", Fig. 1) across the notch in the upper log ("C", Fig. 1). From this line cut a 30° slope to the approximate diameter of the upper log. The notch should now appear as the right hand notch in Photo #7 and may now be rolled onto its seat. The length is still to be scribed.

5

Photo #5. Logs in place.

4

Photo #4. Finished cut on upper log.

As previously stated, this procedure appears complicated but it is not, in fact, at all difficult. It is well suited to axework. A few practice notches should clear up any problems. The notch is very strong and stable and if hewn logs are to be used, it is a style of notch that is well worth considering.

SEALED LAPPED NOTCH

The final notch in this group is a sealed notch. The origin of this notch would appear to have been inspired by a particularly windy winter when even a sawcut could admit too much cold air. It is essentially a flat lapped notch which combines a lock and a step, the step employed to block off the join.

The first cut is a straight lap cut approximately $\frac{1}{4}$ of the log diameter in depth, but 1" to $1\frac{1}{2}$" short of the wall width (Fig. 1). Then cut back to the line leaving a vertical key of an appropriate size. This size will depend on the size of the log but $1\frac{1}{2}$" square would be large enough for a very big log. Next chisel out the lower V, as illustrated in (Fig. 2) The top log is fashioned in much the same way. Cut the lap short, the distance "a", Fig. 2, will be

the amount. In other words, if "a" = 1", then cut the lap 1" short of the final cut at the shoulder. Next cut a recess in the side for the vertical key. Then cut the remainder of the lap away leaving the portion to drop into the V-lock. This notch requires hewn logs -- or, at least hewn to a uniform width on the ends and the bottom portion of each should be shaped to give a uniform cross-section.

To visualize this joint from an armchair situation requires very good three-dimensional perception. One should be a well-advanced builder before attempting to use this notch, or else practice with a model situation until you feel sure you understand it. The challenge lies in obtaining a precision fit at the notch and an equally precise scribed fit along the length. This is done by first cutting the notch and then placing a spacer of equal thickness between the flat portions at each end. Set the scribers to the same width as the thickness of the spacer and complete the scribe. If the work is done well, the fit should be satisfactory.

This notch is for experts and then only for particular applications where the appearance of a lap joint is desired.

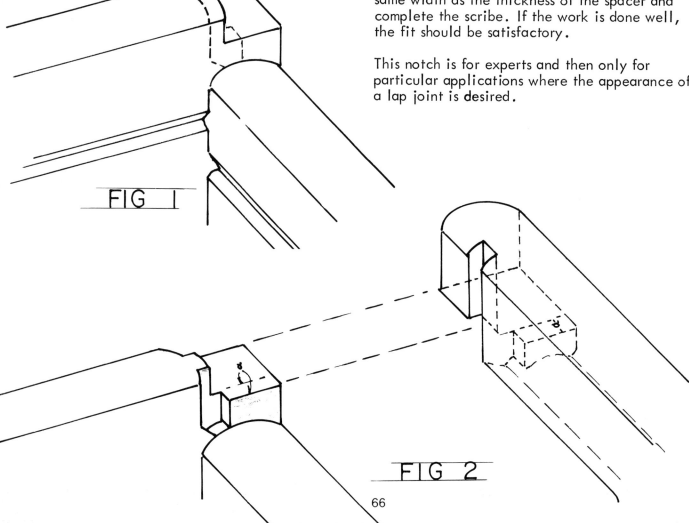

FIG 1

FIG 2

66

FRAMING NOTCHES

MORTISE AND TENON

Timber framing is a great and intricate art. Its neglect began with a Bostonian's invention of balloon framing in the early 19th century, to fill the needs of residential construction in the light of diminishing timber supplies. The steel industry aided in the decline of this ancient art by inventing an assortment of nuts, bolts, and strap iron to speed up heavy construction.

It is generally considered as most unlikely that any rebirth could occur of the timber framing methods such as existed in eastern Canada in the 18th and early 19th centuries. But I find the thought of the timber frame building a most interesting and credible option, even for today, as the cost of plastic, industrialized materials goes up and up while the quality of structures goes down. Someone, I feel sure, if only out of desperation, will surely pick up his axe and build in this grand old way again.

There is a need for a comprehensive book on pièce-en-pièce construction and I hope, one day soon, to do this. Much has been done with respect to historical study, and a great deal of information of a "survey" nature is available in widely scattered publications. But before this is of practical use to today's builder, additional experimental work will have to be completed to adapt pièce-en-pièce forms to present day needs. For versatility and adaptability, this method of building is without peer.

For this particular study of timber joinery, however, I can say that out of these timber framing methods of construction have come a great many timber joins which employ neither bolts nor shear plates, and which the builder will find most useful in a variety of locations. First among these is the mortise and tenon.

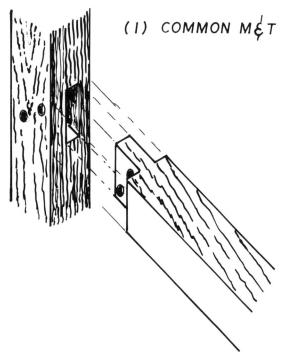

(1) COMMON M&T

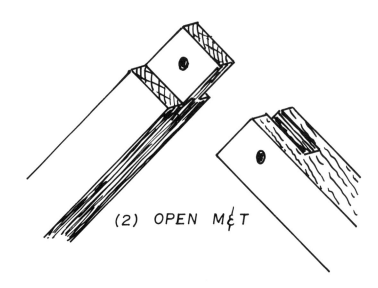

(2) OPEN M&T

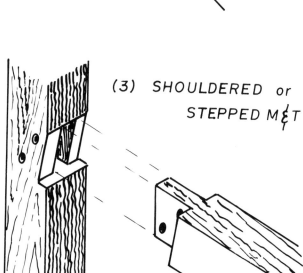

(3) SHOULDERED or STEPPED M&T

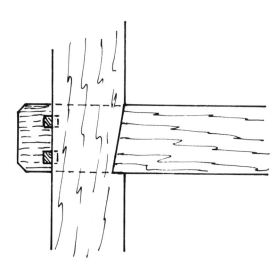

(4) CABINETMAKER'S M&T

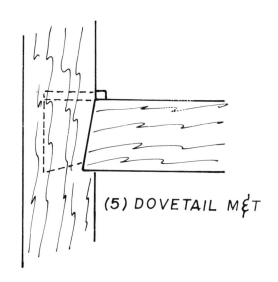

(5) DOVETAIL M&T

FIG 1

The mortise and tenon joint, in one of its many forms, will suit almost any application in wall and roof framing in timber buildings. In particular, roof construction in timber framing offers a whole new world of beauty and spirit for a log house.

A mortise and tenon joint is a square or rectangular recess cut into a timber, with a tenon of similar dimensions to fit into it. There is an infinite variety of kinds, shapes, and uses for this joint. For building purposes, then, let us consider 5 types (Fig. 1):

- common   - open
- stepped   - dovetail
- pinned tennon or cabinet maker's joint

The common mortise and tenon joints would most often be found in compression, i.e., the principal posts in a wall, window posts, interduces (horizontal spacers between principals), struts, and braces.

Open mortise and tenon most often is used to join a pair of common rafters.

Stepped mortise and tenon joints are used for floor joists, beams, and window and door headers which, although weighted, are not under tension.

The pinned mortise and tenon, and the dovetail mortise and tenon, are used for floor joists, collar ties, tie beams, window headers, &c., which are under both weight and tension. If, in the case of a collar tie, the part is not carrying weight, then the step is best omitted.

When used in furniture making, these joints are generally laid out with a try square and a scriber from a prepared face edge.

When heavy timbers or indeed round logs are to be used, the procedure is a little different.

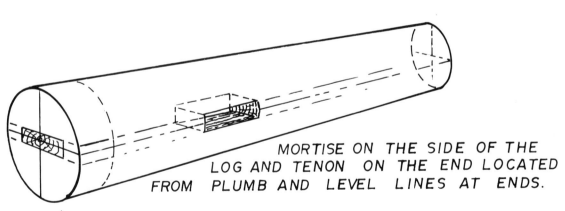

MORTISE ON THE SIDE OF THE LOG AND TENON ON THE END LOCATED FROM PLUMB AND LEVEL LINES AT ENDS.

FIG 2

Method 1: a centre line may be drawn on each end of the timber with a carpenter's level (Fig. 2). Mortises may now be laid out in relation to a chalk line snapped between corresponding points. This will work well for round or hewn logs and even for very crooked logs.

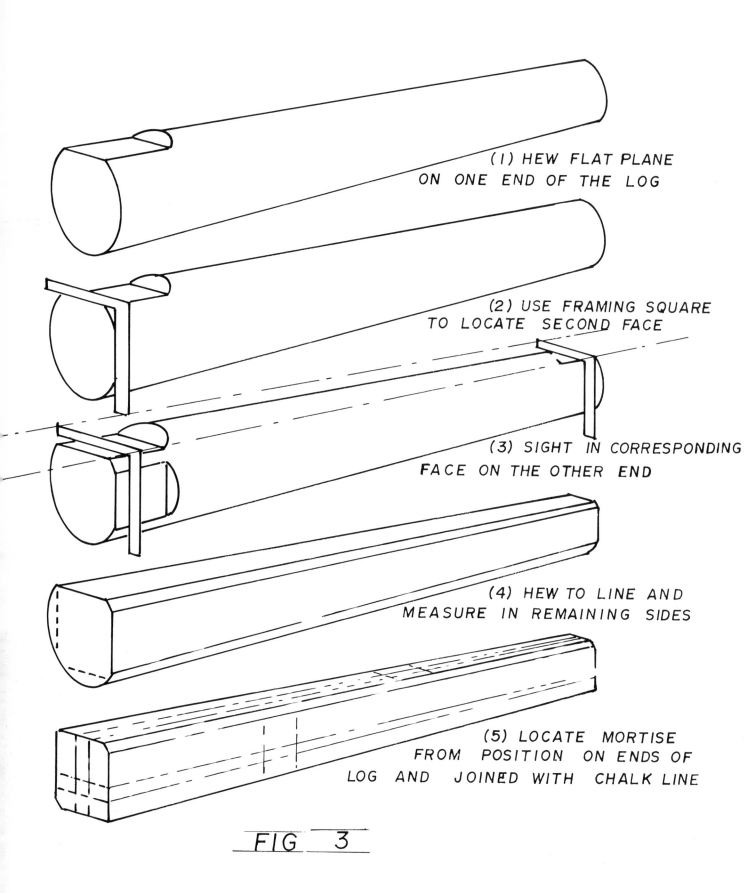

(1) HEW FLAT PLANE ON ONE END OF THE LOG

(2) USE FRAMING SQUARE TO LOCATE SECOND FACE

(3) SIGHT IN CORRESPONDING FACE ON THE OTHER END

(4) HEW TO LINE AND MEASURE IN REMAINING SIDES

(5) LOCATE MORTISE FROM POSITION ON ENDS OF LOG AND JOINED WITH CHALK LINE

FIG 3

Method 2, without a level: hew a short face on one end of the log (1) in Figure 3. Plane this smooth. Hang a framing square over the face to obtain a face at right angles to the first (2). Do the same at the other end, only obtain the first face by "sighting" the square to a second square at the other end (3). Measure in the two remaining sides and then snap a chalk line to obtain a hewing line (4). The location of a mortise should now be measured onto the end of the timber and located by means of a chalk line between ends (5). The reason for this is that hewing is often inaccurate and grave errors occur if measurements are taken from the sides of the material. The success of this type of construction is dependent most strictly upon great accuracy.

In years past, mortises were cut by first boring holes at the ends or corners, with a boring machine. This hand-operated machine would hold the bit at the required angle and the mortise (Fig. 4) could then be cut out with a chisel or a mortising axe.

If the mortise is to extend through the material, carry the dimension lines around and work from both sides. Modern work with electric drills and chain saws often produce bad fits. These tools can be used, but keep the drill size small and work well within the line with the saw. Chain saws are apt to kick back in this application, so it is better to use a small saw -- nothing larger than 4 c.c. displacement.

When the mortise has been roughed in, finish to a square surface along one side and one end with with a mallet and chisel.

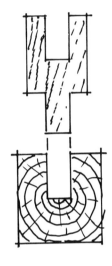

TEMPLATE WILL GAUGE BOTH MORTISE AND TENON

FIG 5

A gauge may be made of a piece of board the same width as the tenon (Fig. 5). Use this as a "feeler" to see that the mortise is of a uniform width.

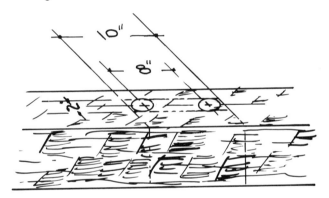

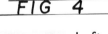

Left: Hand-operated boring machine. Right: Preparing the next log for hewing (at B. Allan Mackie School of Log Building, Prince George).

When the mortise is complete, lay out the tenon in the same manner. Work with a chalk line from the end of the log. The recurring problem in this is to obtain a good clean cut at the shoulder of the tenon.

One way to draw this line is to wrap a piece of heavy paper or similar material 1½ times around the piece of wood. When the edges of the paper are aligned, you are near to the required angle. With square material, you can work from the chalk line joining the ends also.

Cut the tenon accurately. This can be done by sawing to depth at the shoulder, split off the excess wood, then finish with an adze, plane, or slick. Work carefully. Do not do rough work too close to the line, for once the tenon has been cut too small, a great deal of the efficiency of the joint is lost.

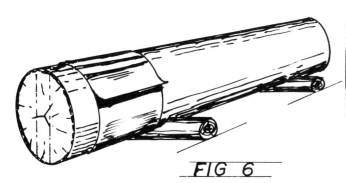

FIG 6

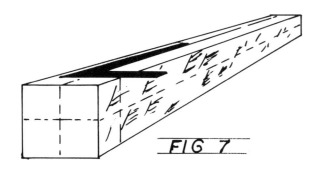

FIG 7

Fig. 6. Obtain a square shoulder on a round log with heavy paper cylinder.

Fig. 7. Square line on hewn log can be obtained with a framing square carefully aligned with a chalk line.

Fig. 8. Mortise and Tenon joints for round log work.

Fig. 9. Draw peg holes in hewn timber.

Fig. 10. Stagger mortises wherever possible.

Fig. 11. White oak peg.

74

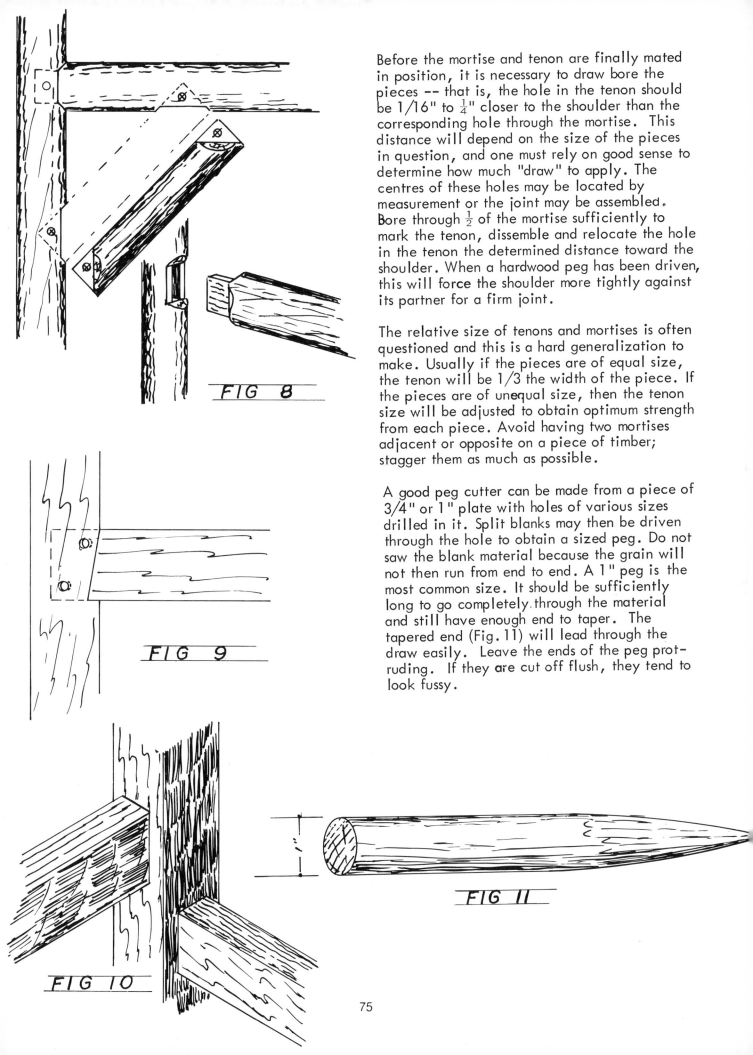

Before the mortise and tenon are finally mated in position, it is necessary to draw bore the pieces -- that is, the hole in the tenon should be 1/16" to $\frac{1}{4}$" closer to the shoulder than the corresponding hole through the mortise. This distance will depend on the size of the pieces in question, and one must rely on good sense to determine how much "draw" to apply. The centres of these holes may be located by measurement or the joint may be assembled. Bore through $\frac{1}{2}$ of the mortise sufficiently to mark the tenon, dissemble and relocate the hole in the tenon the determined distance toward the shoulder. When a hardwood peg has been driven, this will force the shoulder more tightly against its partner for a firm joint.

The relative size of tenons and mortises is often questioned and this is a hard generalization to make. Usually if the pieces are of equal size, the tenon will be 1/3 the width of the piece. If the pieces are of unequal size, then the tenon size will be adjusted to obtain optimum strength from each piece. Avoid having two mortises adjacent or opposite on a piece of timber; stagger them as much as possible.

A good peg cutter can be made from a piece of 3/4" or 1" plate with holes of various sizes drilled in it. Split blanks may then be driven through the hole to obtain a sized peg. Do not saw the blank material because the grain will not then run from end to end. A 1" peg is the most common size. It should be sufficiently long to go completely through the material and still have enough end to taper. The tapered end (Fig. 11) will lead through the draw easily. Leave the ends of the peg protruding. If they are cut off flush, they tend to look fussy.

FIG 8

FIG 9

FIG 10

FIG II

75

DOVETAIL TENON

Dovetail joints used in framing are designed for use where wood is under tension. This will be in collar ties, tie beams, some braces, principal floor joists, and roof trusses.

Collar ties and tie beams are intended to be in tension. Wood has great strength in tension but it is very difficult to use that strength effectively. A dovetail joint can utilize the shear strength of the angled portion only; this runs from 600 to 900 p.s.i. for softwoods and from 700 to 1400 p.s.i. for hardwoods. Therefore, a dovetail joint containing 20 or 30 square inches of effective area may resist 12,000 to 18,000 lbs. of stress.

Dovetail joints used for collar ties are often external (Fig. 12).

The main member should not be cut more than 1/3 of the way through and of the collar tie about 1/3 of the thickness may be cut off. Such dovetails often have only one sloped edge since this is adequate for the application. A dovetail mortise is also effective in this location but is substantially more difficult to cut. This is most often cut as in Fig. 13.

Sufficient space is left above the tenon to permit it to be slid into place, then dropped to its seat. A wedge is driven above the joint "a", Figure 13, to prevent removal and, of course, the joint is also pinned. This is an extremely effective joint for collar ties and upper floor joists where thrust is also expected. The seat of "b", Figure 13, permits full loading of the beams. The lower end of king posts are sometimes secured in this same manner, although that joint is most often simply a 1/3 lap and pegged.

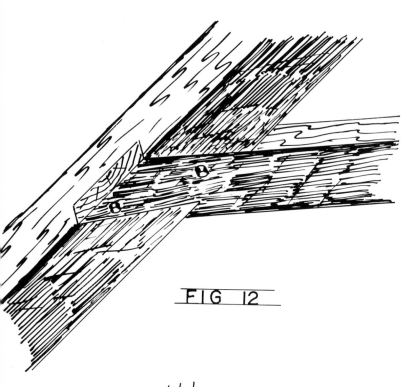

FIG 12

FIG 13

Another effective location for a dovetail joint is in the corner sway brace of framed or log buildings. In this application, the brace crosses the corner flush with the top of the plates (Fig. 14). The combined shoulder and dovetail is an effective brace.

Principal floor joists may be dovetailed into plate timbers or logs, as the case may be. Such a joint usually performs two functions: it carries a load and it acts under tension. The joint is therefore stepped to carry the load and has sufficient dovetail to restrain the thrust (Fig. 15). This layout prevents excessive weakening of the main timber. The apportioning of the amount of wood left under the joint will depend upon the expected loading.

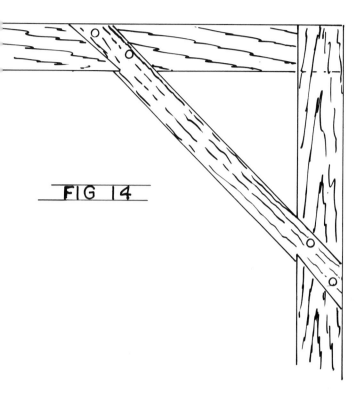

FIG 14

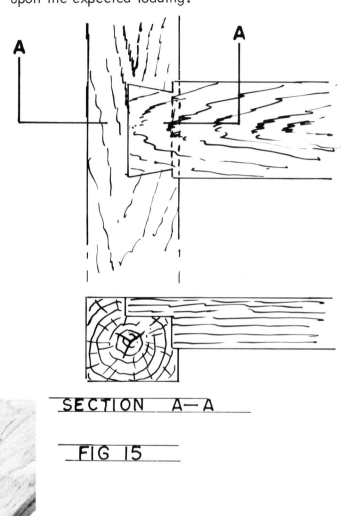

SECTION A—A

FIG 15

Above. Dovetail mortise and tenon as it appears when used for collar tie.

77

RAFTERS

●●

Some joins are under compression. These positions are at the ends of principal rafters, the ends of the purlin braces or struts, any corner bracing, and of course all upright timbers. Purlin braces are either pegged, pinned, or mortised into the principals and king post. The functioning of this fastening is only to retain the position of the piece.

It is important that the compression be as near parallel to the grain as possible, since this is the position in which wood will withstand the greatest stress.

The lower ends of trusses can be stepped in two ways: (1) on top of, or in conjunction with, a tie beam. (2) Directly on or into the wall, the thrust taken up by a collar tie or tie beam which may double as a floor joist. In either case, the end of the principal rafter should bear directly on the wall, unless the lower chord or tie beam is very substantial.

Steps for principal rafter may be as follows in Figure 16.

Example 4 is designed for use where bolts are used. A partial list of bolt sizes appears in Appendix #2, but for larger spans and trusses, the design should be submitted for an engineer's approval (see CANADIAN LOG HOUSE No. 4, p. 64).

In round log construction, it is often difficult to place the lower end of the principal rafter on top of the wall because the remainder of the roof resting on the truss would be above the plate log. In such cases, the following layout is useful (Fig. 17).

The join at the top of the principal rafters is always in compression and requires bolting or pinning only to retain its position.

The classic king post (Fig. 18, "1") may have a short mortise and tenon but no pinning is required after assembly. If the top surfaces are a flat fit, then they should be bolted (Fig. 18, "2"). Log trusses are most generally constructed on the ground and reassembled on the walls. If several identical trusses are to be

assembled, as when each pair of rafters is assembled as a truss to eliminate the need for a continuous ridge and purlins, construct each one directly over a pattern. This pattern may be laid out full size on a loft floor, or the first truss made can become the pattern for each succeeding one. The mortise and tenon joints may again be located with a chalk line but a large T-bevel will assist in obtaining angles (Fig. 19).

Scribed fits are rarely successful for round log ends in truss construction or where posts and beams intersect. They often exhibit the appearance of the final compromise and at best are very slow to produce.

Above. Principal rafter as in (1), Figure 16.

Below. King post as in (1), Figure 18.

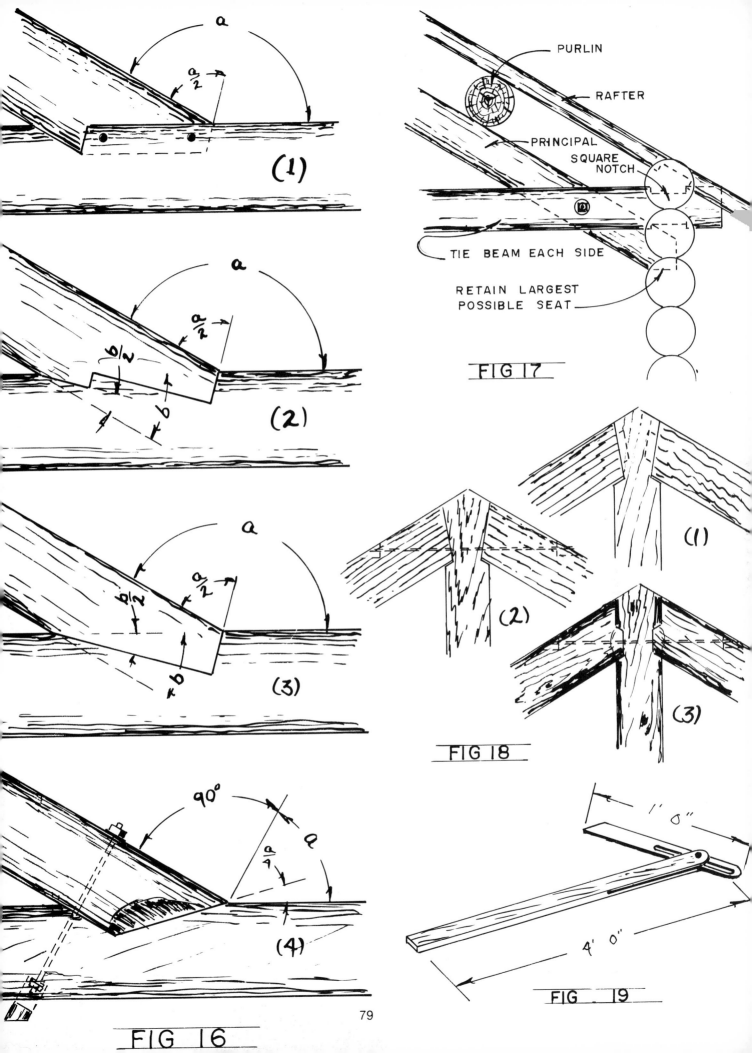

a

$\frac{a}{2}$

(1)

a

$\frac{b}{2}$

b

$\frac{a}{2}$

(2)

a

$\frac{b}{2}$

b

$\frac{a}{2}$

(3)

90°

a

$\frac{a}{4}$

(4)

FIG 16

PURLIN

RAFTER

PRINCIPAL

SQUARE
NOTCH

TIE BEAM EACH SIDE

RETAIN LARGEST
POSSIBLE SEAT

FIG 17

(1)

(2)

(3)

FIG 18

1' 0"

4' 0"

FIG 19

79

A study of framing notches could not be complete without some investigation of common rafter notches and seats for both round log and hewn log construction.

The universally used "bird's mouth" notch for common rafters (1 – Fig. 21) is acceptable for use with dimensional material and where the gable ends are framed. If the gable ends are log, the resultant settling will dislocate the seat and render the joint insecure. In any event, eave blocking is required. In the work done in the past few years, I have avoided the use of eave blocking in preference to setting rafters flush with the top of the plate log (3 and 4 – Fig. 21). Where the rafters are not exposed and a ceiling applied to the underside, almost any of the others will serve. Again, thought must be given to the gable ends and the effect of settling on the rafter seat.

Where a steep roof is used with log rafters, it is sometimes desirable to elevate the eaves in order to admit light to the windows or add headroom at a door. This can be accomplished as in (2), Fig. 21, by removing the lower portion of a 2 x 10 rafter and splicing it onto the top. If log rafters are to be exposed, the rafter may be butted into the plate log (8), Fig. 21, and an overhang applied afterward. If the overhang is short, a scarfed joint securely nailed will do. If the overhang is more properly long, it may be advisable to carry it on an outboard purlin which in turn rests on an extended overrun at the corners and/or on extended ceiling joists acting as camber beams.

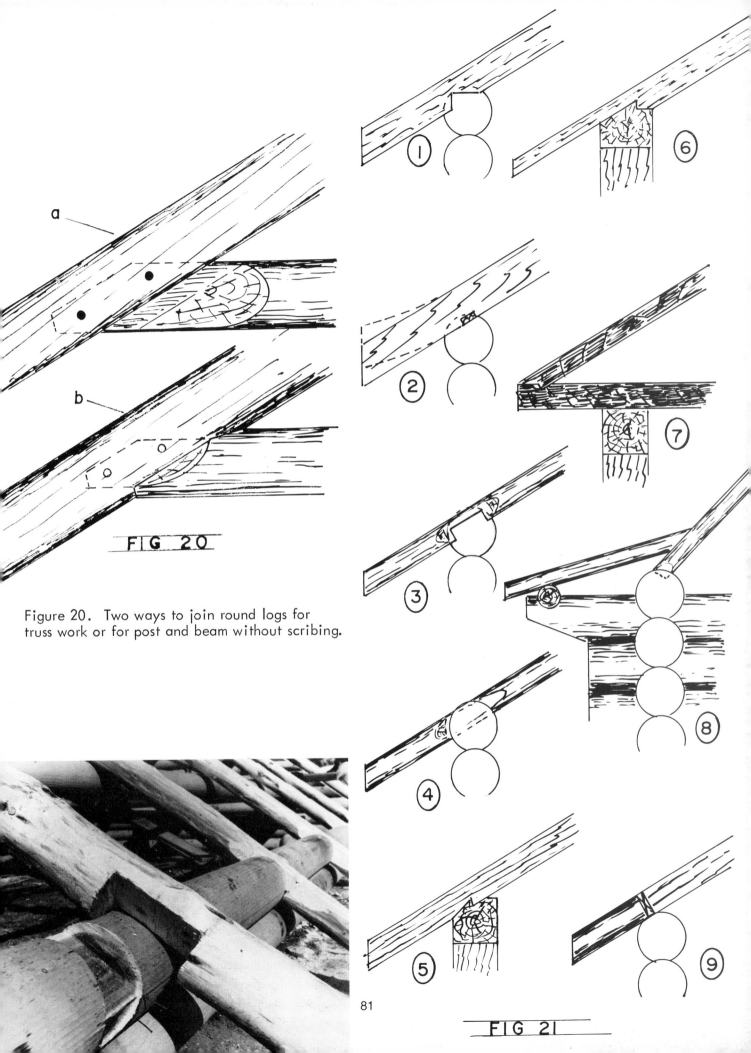

FIG 20

Figure 20. Two ways to join round logs for truss work or for post and beam without scribing.

① ② ③ ④ ⑤ ⑥ ⑦ ⑧ ⑨

FIG 21

SPECIAL NOTCHES

SPLICES

In round log construction, much splicing can be avoided if the design of the building takes into account the quality of the timber available. If the logs available locally are short, then the wall lengths may be arranged to suit this circumstance. In any event, walls should never exceed 20 feet in length without having either an intersecting wall or a stub wall. These serve the important function of providing the necessary stability to the building. In the case of having to utilize short logs, these intersecting walls can be used to good advantage either to hide a splice or to jog the wall and avoid splicing altogether.

I have been taken to see several log buildings that were put up with long, straight walls having no intermediate support. The only limiting factor which seems to have prevailed in the planning was the length of the designer's ruler. In such cases, support had to be added later in the form of partitions or bulkheads or (in one case) timbers strapped to the outside of the wall!

Even with excellent logwork, such a design has no unity with the material. The designer has shown a greater familiarity with concrete blocks than with natural log, and, consequently, the building has taken on the appearance of a concrete block building made of logs. Such a failure in design shows a lack of rapport with

timber as a building material and, while this still happens with larger buildings -- where designers are trained in other materials -- the problem has been largely overcome with smaller residential buildings where the builder has usually taken the time to study the best use of the logs.

The one area of questionable design that still exists in residential construction is the tendency to imitate suburban bungalows or the American ranch style, in logs. In the first instance, the suburban bungalow was designed to make use of highly manufactured material with speed of construction as an objective. The second instance -- the so-called ranch style -- with its sprawling floorplan, is inclined to be unstable. With the addition of support, however, their unusually long walls, too-large windows and glass doors, would become structurally sound. Particularly offensive are those buildings put up with disorderly tiers of logs which have been sawn flat on top and bottom in a sawmill, then spiked together for the purpose of developing a long wall. This practice shows no understanding of the building material and demonstrates a machine-age brutality equalled only by the practice of subjecting the entire tree to machining; these logs are shortened for the convenience of the machine so that the multitude of random splices cries out the sad story of a particular disregard for good workmanship.

Machined and sawn-flat logs have been developed for people wishing to avoid the effort of good design and good workmanship so, like the poor (as the Bible says), "they will always be with us" ... but by definition, they do not form a part of this study of solid timber joinery. It has been mentioned only to indicate that good design will consider the organic nature of the material with even greater emphasis than is given to the expedience of the project. The designer is assured of success if he will make certain that the project embodies these three verities:

FIRMNESS, COMMODITY, AND DELIGHT

Much splicing can be avoided if window and door openings are built in as the walls go up. Short logs can be used between these openings and the available long or straight logs can be saved for use above and below. In a case where a long, unbroken wall is required, logs may be spliced inside an intersecting wall (Fig. 1). If this splice can be used only every second round, so much the better.

When absolutely necessary, logs may be spliced with butt joins, lapped joins, scarfed joins, dovetail joins, and shouldered joins (Fig. 2). The direction in which the join is made -- horizontal or vertical -- will depend on the direction of thrust to which the timber will be subjected. A shouldered join would therefore be used upright as a floor joist, but horizontal as a plate member.

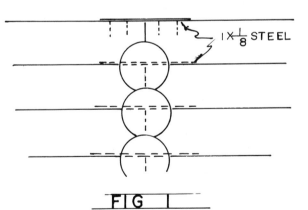

FIG I

Splices in log walls will almost certainly be visible even from a distance and, for this reason, no attempt should be made to camouflage them. By this, I mean: filling in with coloured putty, applying artificial graining to one log in an effort to match it to another, &c. There can be no objection to careful work which has produced a tight, smooth fit and which was undertaken for sound reasons.

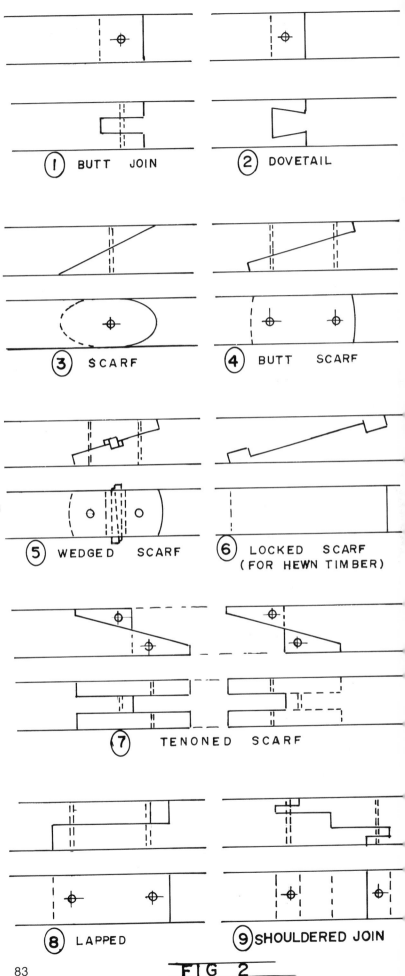

① BUTT JOIN   ② DOVETAIL

③ SCARF   ④ BUTT SCARF

⑤ WEDGED SCARF   ⑥ LOCKED SCARF (FOR HEWN TIMBER)

⑦ TENONED SCARF

⑧ LAPPED   ⑨ SHOULDERED JOIN

FIG 2

WALL INTERSECTION

BLIND NOTCHES

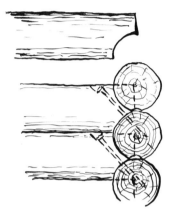

WITH ROUND LOG
CONSTRUCTION—
USE ONE HALF OF
A ROUND NOTCH.
LOG END MUST BE
DRIFTED OR BOLTED.

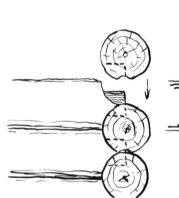 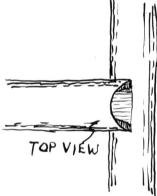

TOP VIEW

DOVETAIL INTERSECTION FOR
ROUND LOGS— THIS NOTCH IS
SLOWER TO BUILD BUT HOLDS
THE LOG MORE FIRMLY.

ADDITIONS

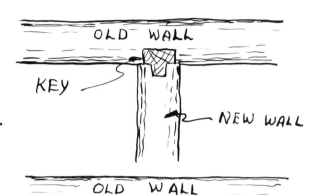

OLD WALL

KEY

NEW WALL

OLD WALL

KEY

NEW WALL

OLD WALL

NEW WALL

INTERSECTION AT
CORNER OF
OLD WALL

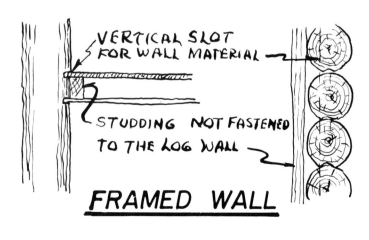

VERTICAL SLOT
FOR WALL MATERIAL

STUDDING NOT FASTENED
TO THE LOG WALL

FRAMED WALL

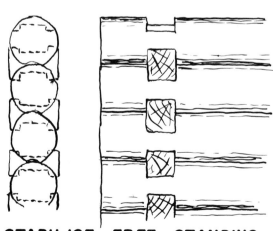

STABILISE FREE STANDING
WALL WITH BLOCKING

ADDITIONS

NOTCHES FOR POSTS

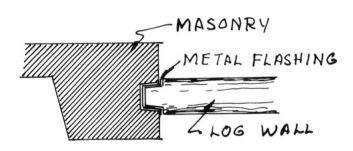

OLD WALL

NEW WALL →

POS. CLOS.

STUB WALL

WHEN A NEW PART IS ADDED A STUB WALL WILL INCREASE STABILITY AND MAY BECOME PART OF THE DESIGN

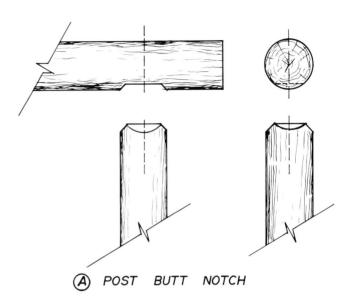

Ⓐ   POST   BUTT   NOTCH

MASONRY

METAL FLASHING

LOG WALL

WHEN ADDING A FIREPLACE WITH AN OUTSIDE FLUE, CUT A MALE KEY ON THE LOG ENDS AND ENCASE THESE ENDS IN A METAL FLASHING SHAPED AS A TROUGH. THIS WILL ALLOW FREE MOVEMENT OF THE LOGS.

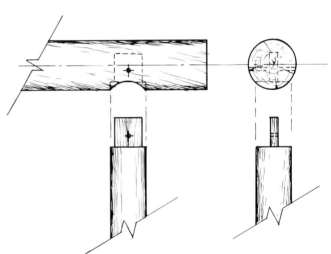

Ⓑ   SCRIBED   MORTICE and TENON

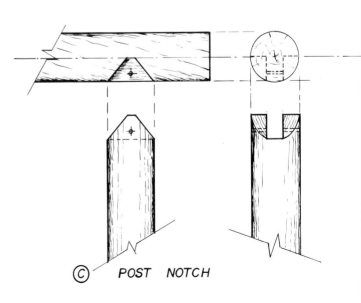

Ⓒ   POST   NOTCH

WINDOW FRAME DETAIL

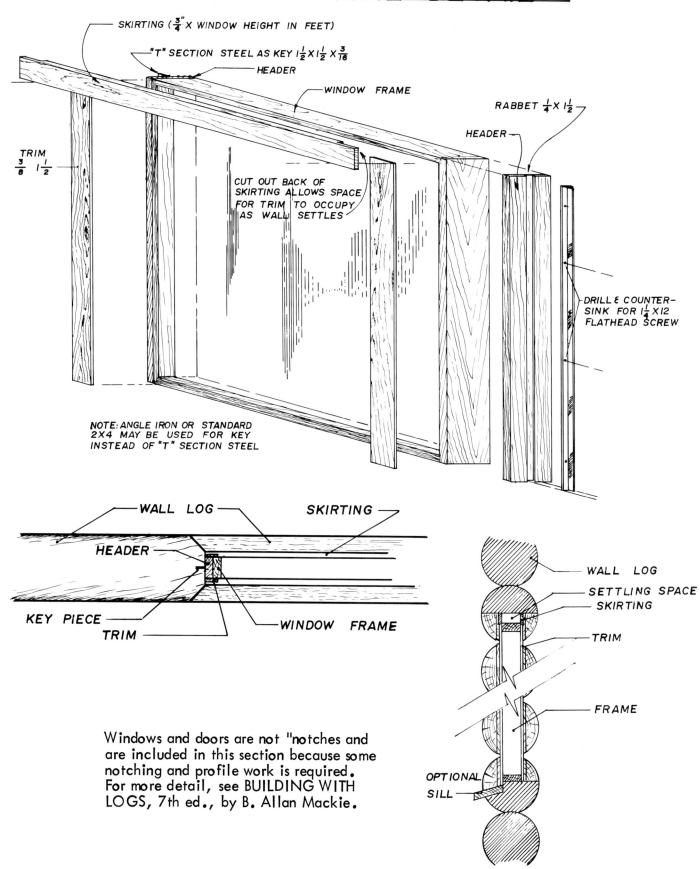

SKIRTING ($\frac{3}{4}$" X WINDOW HEIGHT IN FEET)

"T" SECTION STEEL AS KEY $1\frac{1}{2}$ X $1\frac{1}{2}$ X $\frac{3}{16}$

HEADER

WINDOW FRAME

RABBET $\frac{1}{4}$ X $1\frac{1}{2}$

HEADER

TRIM $\frac{3}{8}$ $1\frac{1}{2}$

CUT OUT BACK OF SKIRTING ALLOWS SPACE FOR TRIM TO OCCUPY AS WALL SETTLES

DRILL & COUNTER-SINK FOR $1\frac{1}{4}$ X 12 FLATHEAD SCREW

NOTE: ANGLE IRON OR STANDARD 2X4 MAY BE USED FOR KEY INSTEAD OF "T" SECTION STEEL

WALL LOG   SKIRTING

HEADER

KEY PIECE

TRIM   WINDOW FRAME

WALL LOG

SETTLING SPACE

SKIRTING

TRIM

FRAME

OPTIONAL SILL

Windows and doors are not "notches and are included in this section because some notching and profile work is required. For more detail, see BUILDING WITH LOGS, 7th ed., by B. Allan Mackie.

86

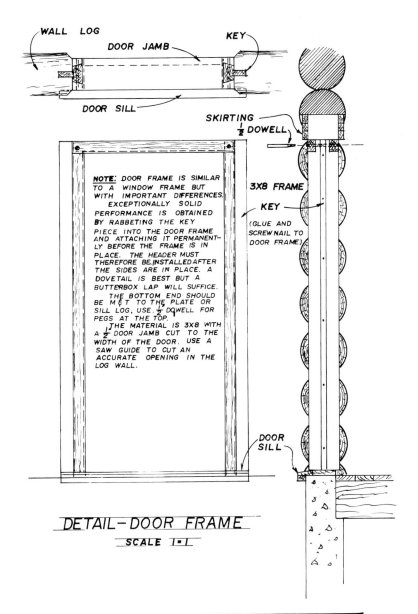

WALL LOG   DOOR JAMB   KEY

DOOR SILL

SKIRTING
½ DOWELL

3X8 FRAME

KEY
(GLUE AND
SCREW NAIL TO
DOOR FRAME)

DOOR SILL

NOTE: DOOR FRAME IS SIMILAR TO A WINDOW FRAME BUT WITH IMPORTANT DIFFERENCES. EXCEPTIONALLY SOLID PERFORMANCE IS OBTAINED BY RABBETING THE KEY PIECE INTO THE DOOR FRAME AND ATTACHING IT PERMANENTLY BEFORE THE FRAME IS IN PLACE. THE HEADER MUST THEREFORE BE INSTALLED AFTER THE SIDES ARE IN PLACE. A DOVETAIL IS BEST BUT A BUTTERBOX LAP WILL SUFFICE.
THE BOTTOM END SHOULD BE MET TO THE PLATE OR SILL LOG, USE ½ DOWELL FOR PEGS AT THE TOP.
THE MATERIAL IS 3X8 WITH A ½ DOOR JAMB CUT TO THE WIDTH OF THE DOOR. USE A SAW GUIDE TO CUT AN ACCURATE OPENING IN THE LOG WALL.

DETAIL-DOOR FRAME
SCALE 1=1

BEAM NOTCH

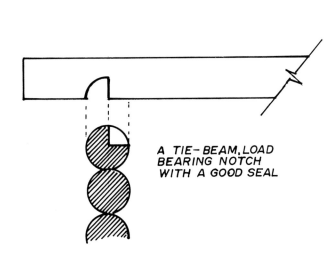

A TIE-BEAM, LOAD BEARING NOTCH WITH A GOOD SEAL

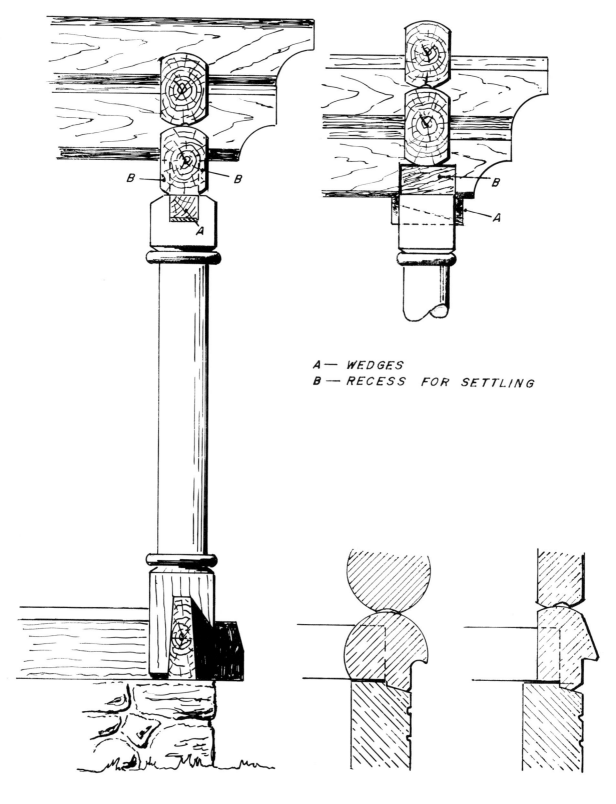

A — WEDGES
B — RECESS FOR SETTLING

PORCH PILLAR   FOUNDATION DRIP SHIELD

88

Appendix

TABLE F

Log Truss Connections

Loading (lbs./ft.)
(Top chord + ½ lower chord)

ROOF PITCH	SPAN	200	400	600	800	1000	1500	2000
4/12	20	C	E	G	H	J		
	25	D	F	H	I	K		
	30	D	G	I	J	K		
	35	E	H	J	K			
	40	E	H	J	K			
6/12	20	A	C	D	F	G	H	J
	25	B	D	E	G	H	I	K
	30	B	D	F	H	H	J	K
	35	C	E	G	H	I	K	
	40	C	E	G	I	J	K	
8/12	20	A	B	C	D	E	G	H
	25	A	B	D	D	E	G	I
	30	A	C	D	E	F	H	I
	35	B	C	E	F	G	I	J
	40	B	D	E	G	H	I	K
10/12	20	A	A	B	C	C	D	F
	25	A	B	B	C	D	E	G
	30	A	B	C	D	D	F	G
	35	A	B	C	D	E	G	H
	40	A	C	D	E	E	G	H
12/12	20	A	A	A	B	B	C	D
	25	A	A	A	B	C	D	E
	30	A	A	B	C	C	D	E
	35	A	A	B	C	D	E	F
	40	A	B	C	C	D	E	G

Detail of Connection

TYPE	Connection 'a' Bolt	Washers	Connection 'b' Bolt	Washers	Connection 'c' Bolt	Washers
A	1/2"(1)	4" dia.				
B	5/8"(1)	5"	5/8"	2" dia.	3/4"	2" dia.
C	3/4"(1)	6"				
D	7/8"(1)	7"				
E	1"(1)	8"	3/4"	2"	7/8"	2¼"
F	3/4"(2)	6"				
G	7/8"(2)	7"				
H	1"(2)	8"	7/8"	2¼"		
I	7/8"(3)	7"			1"	2½"
J	1"(3)	8"	1"	2½"		
K	1"(4)	8"				

LOG ROOF TRUSSES

TABLES SHOWING LOG SIZE FOR VARIOUS TRUSS SPANS AND LOADINGS*

(Valid for Any Pitch of Roof)

1. TOP CHORD

TRUSS SPAN	TOP CHORD LOADING** (LBS./LIN. FT.)						
	200	400	600	800	1000	1500	2000
	LOG DIAMETER (INCHES)						

1. TOP CHORD

		200	400	600	800	1000	1500	2000
Table A	20'	6.9	8.8	10.1	11.0	11.9	13.8	15.4
Use for	25'	8.1	10.3	11.7	12.8	13.8	15.8	17.4
simple &	30'	9.1	11.5	13.2	14.5	15.6	17.9	19.7
single-	35'	10.2	12.7	14.6	16.1	17.3	19.8	21.8
post	40'	11.2	14.0	15.9	17.6	18.9	21.7	23.8
Table B	20'	4.4	5.5	6.4	7.2	8.1	10.0	11.5
Use for	25'	5.1	6.5	7.3	8.2	9.1	11.1	12.8
King &	30'	5.7	7.2	8.3	9.2	10.0	12.2	14.1
Fink	35'	6.4	8.1	9.2	10.1	11.0	13.0	14.8
trusses	40'	6.9	8.8	10.1	11.0	11.9	13.8	15.4

2. LOWER CHORD

	LOWER CHORD LOADING (LBS./LIN. FT.)						
	100	200	300	400	600	800	1000
	LOG DIAMETER (INCHES)						

2. LOWER CHORD

		100	200	300	400	600	800	1000
Table C	20'	8.8	11.2	12.7	14.0	16.0	17.6	18.9
Use for	25'	10.4	12.8	14.7	16.2	18.5	20.4	22.0
simple	30'	12.0	14.5	16.6	18.2	20.9	23.0	-
truss	35'	13.4	16.0	18.4	20.3	23.2	-	-
only	40'	14.8	17.7	20.1	22.2	-	-	-
Table D	20'	5.6	6.9	8.0	8.8	10.0	11.0	11.9
Use for	25'	6.4	8.1	9.3	10.3	11.7	12.8	13.8
single-	30'	7.2	9.1	10.5	11.5	13.2	14.5	15.6
post &	35'	8.0	10.2	11.6	12.7	14.6	16.1	17.3
King	40'	8.8	11.2	12.7	14.0	16.0	17.6	18.9
Table E	20'	4.2	5.2	6.0	6.6	7.6	8.5	9.2
Use for	25'	4.8	6.2	6.5	7.7	8.9	9.8	10.6
Fink	30'	5.5	7.0	8.0	8.8	10.1	11.1	12.0
truss	35'	6.2	7.7	8.9	9.8	11.2	12.3	13.2
	40'	6.7	8.4	9.7	10.6	12.2	13.4	14.4

*Tables prepared for S-P-F species   ** Top chord loading is horizontal lbs./ft.

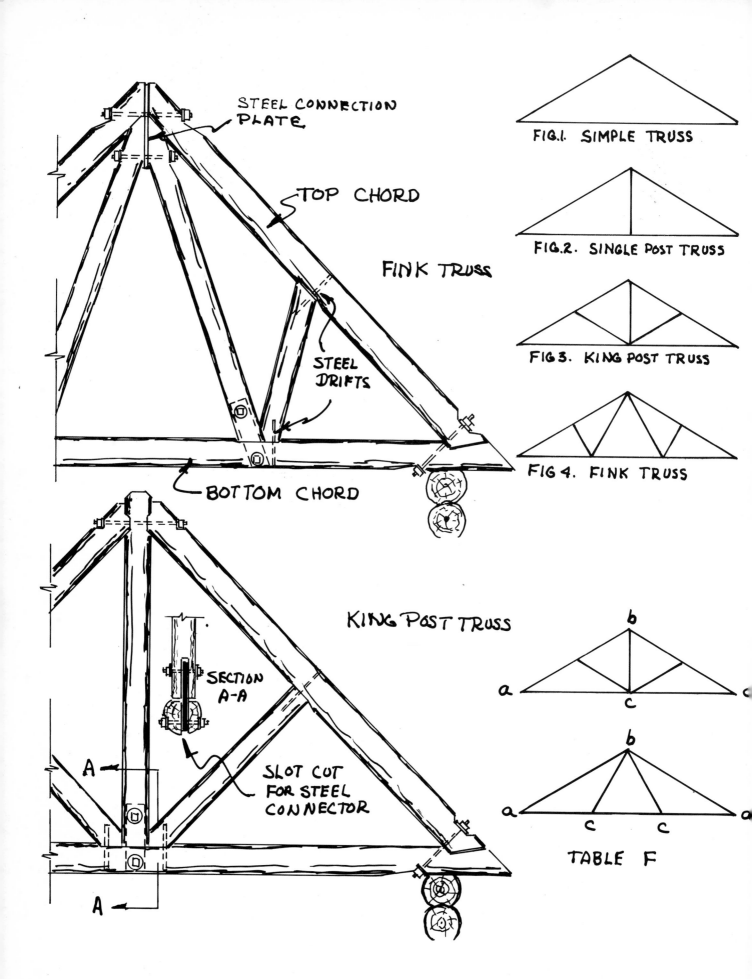

STEEL CONNECTION PLATE

TOP CHORD

FINK TRUSS

STEEL DRIFTS

BOTTOM CHORD

FIG.1. SIMPLE TRUSS

FIG.2. SINGLE POST TRUSS

FIG 3. KING POST TRUSS

FIG 4. FINK TRUSS

KING POST TRUSS

SECTION A-A

A

SLOT CUT FOR STEEL CONNECTOR

A

b

a c c

b

a c c a

TABLE F